THE SOCIAL STUDIES SOURCEBOOK

THE SOCIAL STUDIES SOURCEBOOK
Ideas for Teaching in the Elementary and Middle School

Frank L. Ryan
University of California, Riverside

KLINCK MEMORIAL LIBRARY
Concordia Teachers College
River Forest, Illinois 60305

ALLYN AND BACON, INC.
Boston, London, Sydney, Toronto

Copyright © 1980 by Allyn and Bacon, Inc., 470 Atlantic Avenue, Boston, Massachusetts 02210. All rights reserved. No part of the material protected by this copyright notice may be reproduced or utilized in any form or by any means, electronic or mechanical, including photocopying, recording, or by any information storage and retrieval system, without written permission from the copyright owner.

Library of Congress Cataloging in Publication Data

Ryan, Frank L
  The social studies sourcebook.

  Bibliography: p.
  Includes index.
  1. Social sciences—Study and teaching (Secondary)—United States. 2. Social sciences—Study and teaching (Elementary)—United States. I. Title.
H62.R96   372.8'3'044   79–20320
ISBN 0–205–06802–2

Printed in the United States of America.

To

*Sandy, Scott, Lance, Leslie,
and Jennifer*

CONTENTS

Preface   *xi*
Using the Book   *xiii*

1 SKILLS   1

Rationale   2

THINKING PROCESSES   2
Rationale
   Observing   3
   Grouping/Categorizing/Classifying   14
   Comparing/Relating   24
   Predicting/Hypothesizing/Educated
     Guessing   36
   Displaying Predictions   45
   Inferring   49

STUDENT RESEARCH   60
Rationale   60
   Other Research Ideas   62

viii CONTENTS

        Other Rank-Order Ideas   *64*
        Mode, Mean, Range   *69*
        Other Experimental Research Ideas   *72*

    INFORMATIONAL SKILLS   75
    Rationale   75
        Locating Information   *75*
        Gathering and Organizing
          Information   *80*
        Collecting Original Information   *85*
        Processing Information   *92*
        Reporting   *98*

    MAPS, GLOBES, SPACE
      UTILIZATION   *102*
    Rationale   *102*
        Activities   *102*

    TIME AND CHRONOLOGY   *115*
    Rationale   *115*
        Activities   *115*

2 CONCEPTS   125

    Rationale   *125*
        Rules   *127*
        Conflict   *131*
        Goods/Services   *134*
        Learning   *139*
        Technology   *161*

3 TOPICS OF STUDY   171

    Rationale   *171*
        Career Education   *172*

Future/Change 183
Consumer Education 200
Advertising 213
Global Education 229
School 237
News/Newspapers 255
Human Equality 267
Environmental Education 277

4 AFFECTIVE/EVALUATIVE DOMAIN 285

Rationale 285
Affective/Evaluative Activities 287

Cross-Index of Activities 298

PREFACE

The ideas presented in this book represent the culmination of nineteen years of reflecting, learning, and interacting and discussing with others about what specifically happens during social studies instruction that is potentially significant for the learner.

It has been my impression that many social studies textbooks are primarily devoted to presenting rationales for various instructional topics, strategies, and themes; with only spasmodic, almost apologetic, injections of how the "theory" translates into specific classroom applications. One result is that the readers of such books are often left confused concerning what it is they must *specifically* do in the classroom in order to have learners "discover," "process," "inquire," or dwell on the "affective."

If my impressions are accurate then we might have at least a partial explanation of why so many teachers can glibly speak in general, even supportive, terms about various "good" instructional procedures and at the same time fail to reflect the specifics in their own classroom practices.

Thus, my premise in establishing the format for this book was that the reader would benefit most by receiving specific suggestions for carrying out meaningful classroom instructional activity. But although I have emphasized instructional specifics, I am also hopeful that I have presented sufficient evidence to convince the reader that a series of rationales were imposed on my selections and on my ordering of the ideas presented.

The emphasis in this book is on an explicit presentation of nearly 500 classroom applications of current social studies instructional "thinking." I have assumed that the reader has acquired, or is in the process of acquiring, knowledge of current instructional trends and is in need of specific examples of classroom applications. It is my hope that at least two results will follow for the reader and *user* of this book: greater understanding of the instructional topics I have chosen as content organizers, and, maybe more importantly, an enthusiastic commitment to integrate current instructional trends into personal classroom practices.

Many people contributed directly as well as indirectly to my thinking as I compiled the ideas for this book, including Connie Wagner, San Diego City Schools, Lee and Charlotte Anderson, Northwestern University, David King, author and consultant, Margaret Branson, Holy Names and Mills College, Art Ellis, University of Minnesota, Bill Joyce, Michigan State University, Ron Wheeler, College of William and Mary, and Dan Donlan and Rob McKeown, University of California, Riverside. Certainly, other colleagues have made contributions and collectively I am also indebted to them.

Finally, I would like to thank Steve Mathews, editor, Allyn and Bacon, for his continuous support and patience during the preparation of the manuscript. My thanks also to Grace Sheldrick for her skillful handling of the details of production.

F. L. R.

USING THE BOOK

Use of the many instructional suggestions contained in this book may be approached in at least two ways.

1. To improve existing social studies units of study and materials.

2. As a source of mini-units of study, by selecting ideas from within a particular section or by combining ideas from several sections. For example, the ideas suggested for the concept *learning* (Section 2, *Concepts*) might be combined with those suggestions for the topic, *school* (Section 3, *Topics of Study*). Similarly, activities suggested for the concept *communication* (Section 2) might be combined with those for the topic *news* (Section 3), *working with information* (Section 1, *Skills*) and *observing* (Section 1).

A further note on combining ideas from various sections of the book might be in order. Typically, developers of social studies curricular materials pay homage to three main sets of objectives: skills, understandings (such as topics of study, concepts) and the affective domain. Note that each of these categories of objectives is represented through various sections in this sourcebook. Thus, when implementing a suggestion from a particular section, the teacher can look for related ideas from other sections, with the aim of involving students in multiple, versus singular, instructional objectives.

The specific ideas presented in *The Social Studies Sourcebook* can also be used to update current instructional efforts. For example, we may hear of such topics as career education or consumer education, but fail to incorporate their substance into our teaching. The specific way in which the activities have been presented here should facilitate their application and integration into existing instructional procedures.

It is intended that the various 477 activities be used with on-going units of study, textbooks, library books, and other sources typically available. Therefore, the various activities described do not collectively form the total social studies program or even necessarily reflect a rationale for one; rather, the activities here are indicative of topics found in newer or evolving social studies curricula.

Ordinarily, the instructional procedures needed for implementing a specific activity are woven into a description of the activity. Elaboration of instructional strategies reflected in the many activities described may be found in such social studies textbooks as those listed below.

Ellis, Arthur K. *Teaching and Learning Elementary Social Studies.* Boston: Allyn and Bacon, 1977.

Jarolimek, John. *Social Studies in Elementary Education.* New York: Macmillan, 1977.

Joyce, William W., and Frank L. Ryan. *Social Studies and the Elementary Teacher: Promises and Practices.* Washington, D.C.: National Council for the Social Studies, 1977.

Michaelis, John U. *Social Studies for Children in a*

Democracy: Recent Trends and Developments. Englewood Cliffs, N.J.: Prentice-Hall, Inc., 1976.

Oliner, Pearl M. *Teaching Elementary Social Studies: A Rational and Humanistic Approach.* New York: Harcourt, Brace, Jovanovich, 1977.

Preston, Ralph C., and Wayne L. Herman Jr. *Teaching Social Studies in the Elementary School.* New York: Holt, Rinehart & Winston, 1974.

Ryan, Frank L. *Exemplars for the New Social Studies.* Englewood Cliffs, N.J.: Prentice-Hall, Inc., 1971.

Welton, David A., and John T. Mallan. *Children and Their World: Teaching Elementary Social Studies.* Chicago: Rand McNally, 1977.

Section 1

SKILLS

RATIONALE

It is most appropriate to begin a book like this one with skills activities. Even momentary reflection can lead us to conclude that the use of the kinds of skills delineated in this section, especially those skills dealing with thinking processes, extends beyond our school experiences to permeate all facets of our lifelong activities and pursuits.

The implementation of skills activities should be thought of as an integrative, versus isolated, aspect of our instructional efforts. Skills instruction takes place within the context of the subject matter and attitudinal objectives we are also pursuing. Furthermore, regardless of the topics of study or the set of concepts introduced, teachers can ordinarily weave into their lessons instructional strategies that provide for learner growth in a variety of skill areas, such as those reflected in the activities that follow.

THINKING PROCESSES

RATIONALE

Thinking processes can serve a critical coordinating and educational role in any social studies instruction. Instructional uses of thinking processes might include an involvement of students in *guessing* how life might be different if most people were able to retire at age forty; *comparing* their schools with those their parents attended; and *categorizing* different kinds of tools found in the classroom. In each of these processing activities, the participant is required intellectually to reshape (that is, to process) his or her existing knowledge.

Traditionally, students have been placed into nonprocessing roles, in which knowledge is assimilated and then returned (during, for example, a class discussion or a test) in essentially the same form as received. A teacher familiar with "process possibilities" can easily and quickly inject a "predicting activity" or a "comparing activity" (or similar process) into a faltering instructional environment and probably inject it with some renewed sense of life. Even the least imaginative, the dullest, and most listless social studies instruction can be at least partially salvaged for the students if they are called on to "do something" with the lesson's content (to impose thinking processes) rather than just to receive it without comment.

A constant search for opportunities to integrate thinking processes into all social studies activity can appeal to our instructional intuitions from several vantage points. First, thinking processes have a wide range of instructional applications that can permeate *any* topic of study and *any* emphasis within that topic. The instructional situation is rare indeed that cannot be enhanced through student involvement with a thinking process or two.

Secondly, provision for thinking processes in a lesson provides opportunities for students to act both within and on their learning experiences rather than to be relegated to the role of passive receptors. For example, in using the thinking processes, students do not read about classifications, they classify; nor do they listen to the predictions of other people to the exclusion of making their own.

Finally, our every day activity frequently demands that we swiftly and smoothly employ various thinking processes as we strive to impose sense, order, and meaning into our lives. Daily we are forced to sift and sort through the countless sensations that flood our life space and attempt to establish meaningful relationships between otherwise disparate pieces. It is with total confidence that we can forecast that the present necessity for such processing behavior will be at least as vital to participants in the twenty-first century as it is to those of us currently sifting and sorting through the phenomena of today's world.

Instructional applications are given for the following thinking processes: observing, grouping/categorizing/classifying, comparing/relating, predicting/hypothesizing/educated guessing, and inferring. Note that in most instances multiple terms have been clustered into a single process category (such as grouping/categorizing/classifying) since the instructional applications are easily relatable.

The thinking process categories presented are not the only nor necessarily the "best" ones available for instructional applications; rather, they are representative of the categories commonly found in process-oriented curricula. Formal definitions for the process categories are not given, for it is felt that the aura of meaning surrounding each can easily be induced from the many examples presented.

Observing

1 *Mood Observing*

You, or a student, show the expression of someone who is:

    a. Mad   b. Happy   c. Sad

Figure 1

Ask students to describe what they saw that allowed them to "know" what mood was being enacted. See Figure 1.

☼ 2 *Shoe Box Observations*

Place several different objects (such as a rock, a piece of chalk, an eraser, a small book, a ball) into a shoe box. Then blindfold students and ask them to withdraw one object at a time. After they identify each object, ask the students to name the characteristics of the object they were able to observe and to name which senses they used.

☼ 3 *Recess Observing*

Ask two students to work independently and observe what happens on a section of the playground (or cafeteria or hall) during a recess. The students could jot down ideas, but this is not vital to this activity. Have the students report separately to the class. Compare the two sets of observations and discuss the possible reasons for any variations.

4 *Observing Related Phenomena*

Identify one broad observational category, then have students note all related phenomena within a specific location. For example, the broad classification could be *paper*. Have the students name (list, if they possess the requisite skills) all products made of paper in their classroom. Wood, plastic, cloth, and metal are other examples of observational categories that might be used.

5 *Observing Out-of-School*

Note to Activity 4: Not only various school rooms can be observed; but also consider sending selected students to nearby businesses. For example, students might observe all the uses of paper at a fast-food franchise and then use these data to make predictions regarding the impact of increased paper use and consumption on other uses of trees and tree products.

6 *Observation Grids*

Set up an *observation grid* to help students record their observations. See Figure 6 for an example of a grid used by a group of students while looking for instances of paper product use in a fast-food restaurant.

Activity	Paper Use
Eating	Food wrapping, plate, table mat, straws, straw wrappers
Writing	Order pad
Cleaning	Napkin, towels

Observational items can be added to the activity column (such as reading, relaxing), or additional use columns can be added (such as metal, plastic, wood). Try to use

6   SECTION 1

Figure 6

few categories at first and consider using drawings or pictures to indicate the observational categories.

☼ 7 *Observing Other Classrooms*

Have students visit other classrooms to observe what is in the rooms. For example, students can note what furniture is present: its size, shape, location, quantity, how it is being used; what instructional materials and aids are available: globes, maps, books, aquariums, charts, pictures, and their location and use.

☼ 8 *Combining Observations with Other Thinking Processes*

Consider using another thinking process (comparing/relating) with Activity 7. For example, have the students use the same observational categories to collect data in their room and in another room. Then, using the data collected, compare the rooms:

> How is our furniture alike/different from that found in Room X?
> Why are there differences?
> What is the connection between these differences and what usually takes place in these classrooms?

9 *What Do You See?*

Any time you display, hold up, or distribute any materials, consider first asking the nonfocused question: What do you see? Frequently, through our initial questions we ask students to focus in on specific things that can be observed (such as, Where is the river located that is shown in the picture?), thereby eliminating, or short--circuiting, other possibilities for students to make observations.

Follow-up questions can then be used to cull out those observations that best serve the instructional thrust for a particular lesson.

10 *What Has Changed?*

Occasionally change something from the "usual" in the classroom and ask the students to detect any differences. Some possibilities:

> Remove a light bulb
> Place construction paper over a window pane
> Leave your coat on
> Place furniture, such as your desk, in a slightly different position
> Change the arrangement on a display table, or alter an existing arrangement
> Place new books on the shelves

SECTION 1

Move the trash cans to a different location
Write with a different color chalk

11 *Observational Bingo*

The materials required for this activity can be easily created and are reusable.

Materials needed

A. Generate a stack of about 30 "observation cards" by entering observation categories on 3 × 5 index cards (1 category per card). Examples of observation categories that can be used include:

> Something in the room that begins with the letter *R* (. . . *M*, . . . *S*, . . . etc.)
> A living thing
> Something that is yellow (. . . green, . . . red, . . . etc.)
> Something that has yellow and green in it (. . . blue and yellow, . . . white and black, . . . etc.)
> Something that is longer than the teacher (. . . longer than you are)
> Something that is smaller than you
> Something that is smaller (larger) than you and is alive
> Something that is smaller (larger) than you and is never moved
> Something that is smaller (larger) than you and is used during reading
> Something that is as soft as a sponge
> Something as hard as a rock
> Something that tears as easily as paper, but is not paper
> Something that has been added to our classroom since school began
> Something we had in our classroom but is now gone
> Something we have in our classroom that is not found in (name another) classroom

Something in our classroom (other than a person) that has grown bigger since school began

Something as smooth as a desk top, but not a desk top

Something as slippery as a fish, but not a fish

Something that is sharp like a thumbtack, but not a thumbtack

Something heavier (lighter) than your desk

Someone in the classroom who is taller (shorter) than you

Place the stack of cards in a shoe box.

B. Using tag board or index cards, cut out five squares approximately 2″ × 2″. Number the cards 1 through 5 and place them in a shoe box.

C. Make bingo cards of approximately 4″ × 6″ from tag board, as shown in Figure 11.

Create from three to five different number configurations by randomly pulling numbers out of the box (see B, above) and making the assignment to the next square on the card. Rather than print each card separately, make a ditto master for the varied number configurations, run it off, and staple it to a piece of chip or tag board.

D. Give each player fifteen chips of construction paper, each one the size of a number square on the card.

5	4	4	1
3	Free	3	5
4	3	1	2
5	2	5	1

Figure 11

10   SECTION 1

Play of the game

Someone pulls and announces a number (see B, above) and then pulls and announces an "observation card" (see A, above). The first three people to raise their hands who have the announced number uncovered on their card are allowed to respond. Turns are taken in responding. A person can not use an observation already used for that particular category (however, the same object could be used for a different category).

Suggestion: Select a group of three students to serve as judges on the acceptability of responses in terms of correctness and repetition.

The first person to form a straight line of answers across any two sides of the card wins the game.

The game can be played on an individual basis, or groups of students can team together to play a single card and cooperatively assist one another.

Consider involving the students in creating additional observational categories.

12   *Bean Bag Observations*

A team of three students position themselves throughout any section of the classroom. One team member is given a bean bag (or chalk eraser or similar object). An observation card (see the description of Activity 11, *Observational Bingo*) is drawn and announced. The bean bag is then passed among the team members and placed on an object that fits the description on the observational card. However, team members may not talk to one another (motioning is allowable), nor move more than two steps *while holding* the bean bag. The turn is immediately terminated if anyone talks, takes more than two steps while holding the bean bag, makes a misapplication, or drops the bean bag.

Two scoring procedures can be applied: (1) Use a

stop watch to time the teams' "observations"; or, (2) Allow each team 60 seconds to make its choice and award one point for a correct placement. The team with the best (lowest) time or most points is the winner.

13 *Scavenger Observation*

The game requires a set of about ten scavenger observation items, requiring students to make specific identifications of varied phenomena around the school. For example, students might be asked to locate the following people or things:

> Bulletin boards that include children's work
> Someone helping another person
> Children playing a game using a ball
> Children playing, but not using a ball
> Teachers visiting with other teachers
> A student lying down
> Someone teaching who is not a regular teacher
> Someone using a telephone
> Someone using a typewriter
> Something needing repairs
> Something needing to be cleaned
> Something new
> Something useful for moving books between rooms
> A sign that would help a visitor to the school

Several procedures can be used to disseminate the observation items: ditto a list of about five to ten items and distribute or enter each item on a 3″ × 5″ index card (making multiple copies), shuffle the resulting deck, and deal out five or so cards to each observer.

Allow the observers to work in teams of two. Allow each team to report to the others on their observations.

Note

Rather than having everyone in your class make their observations simultaneously, you may want to send only one or several observation-pairs out at a time.

14 Observation Interest Center

Activity 13, *Scavenger Observation,* with some minor modifications, can be incorporated into an interest center activity. Observations can be confined to the classroom and reviewed with the teacher or an aide.

Another evaluative possibility is to have lists available of what might be observed in the classroom that is appropriate for each of the observation cards and to have the students make comparisons with their own observations, as well as locate the additional observational possibilities listed that they did not make.

15 Team Observation

Using a deck of observation cards (see Activity 11, *Observational Bingo*), deal out ten to fifteen cards along a chalk tray, with the blank side showing. Divide the class into two teams. A member from one of the teams selects a card, makes the observational identification called for, and then shares the card with a panel of three students who decide on the appropriateness of the response. Each appropriate response earns one point for the contributing member's team. In alternate fashion, all team players take a turn.

16 Team Observation—Timed

Alternate procedure for Activity 15: Deal out five cards. Have a pair of students make all observations called for as quickly as possible. The student pair with the fastest time is the winner.

17 Reaction Observation

Place into a paper sack various items, such as: a candy bar, a ball point pen, a rock, a new pencil, etc. Explain to the class that people will be selected to draw objects from the bag that may be kept. Without announcing it to the rest of the class, select three to five students to mark on separate data sheets (see Figure 17) how each student appeared after drawing a "gift" from the bag. Afterwards share and compare the results.

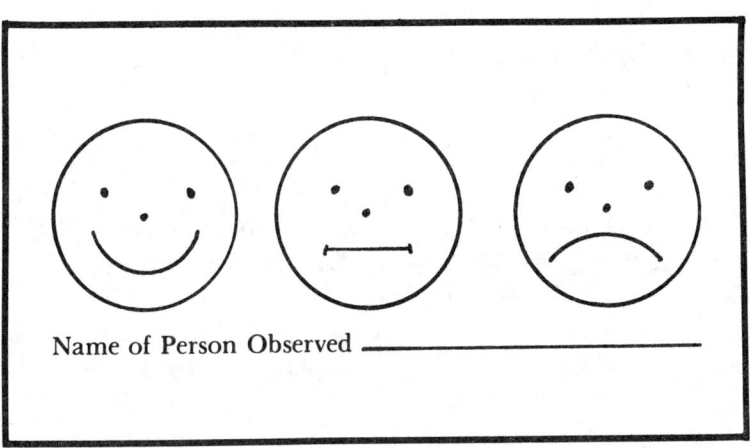

Figure 17

18 Observing Without Eyes

Visit familiar locations in the school and ask the students to list observations using several of their senses. For example, go to the cafeteria and have them list everything they can see. (Younger students can tape record their observations). Then have the students close their eyes and observe and list what they can hear, and then, what they can smell.

19 Blind Identification

A spinoff of Activity 18 is to blindfold students and move them to a familiar school location (such as the cafeteria, gym, office, entrance, or parking lot). Then ask the students to identify the location as well as the "observable" information they found useful in making the identification. Have the students also identify the senses they used for their observations.

Grouping/Categorizing/Classifying

20 Grouping Classroom Observations

List everything on the chalk board that the students can observe in the classroom within a short period of time, such as two minutes. Then have them think of categories that begin to classify the listed data. If the class has difficulty, then offer a few suggestions and have them make the applications (such as hard, soft, alive, not alive, made of metal, made from cloth, learning, playing, etc.).

21 Classmate Categories

Have the students observe others in their class and think of categories that include certain classmates.

Note

In this case, try to elicit categories that exclude as well as include. Thus, the category *7th graders* used for a room with only 7th graders in it would not be used).

Possibilities include

1. Boys, girls
2. Last names begin with a letter from A to M

SKILLS   15

3. Birthdays in January (or February, etc.)
4. Left-handed
5. Shorter than me; taller than me
6. Saw the movie, "_____"

22   The Categories Game

Different categories are written on separate index cards.

Examples:

Animals	Colors
Cities	Flowers
States	Trees
Cars	Sports
Oceans	Movies
Dogs	TV programs
Clothes	Numbers
Food	Furniture
Famous people	

The game is played in pairs. The cards are shuffled and one member draws about five cards. The other member of the pair sits facing the partner but with his or her back to the class. After the cards are shown to the class, the member with the cards selects one and gives several appropriate items for the category (such as red, blue, green for the category colors). The partner guesses at the category written on the card. Any number of cues can be given, but all of the cards are to be guessed in a predetermined amount of time (such as one and one-half minutes).

23   City Characteristics

List a series of items around a broad topic that your class has been studying (such as cities, modes of transportation, states, products, services). Think of several classification descriptors for that specific topic. Make multiple copies of the topical items and classifications and distribute them. Have the students enter as many classifications as they think they can support after each topic listed.

Example

Topic: Cities

Los Angeles _____
Seattle _____
Duluth _____
Fargo _____
Kansas City _____
Denver _____
Buffalo _____
Miami _____
Atlanta _____

Classifications

A.	Capital	F.	Midwestern
B.	Within the same state	G.	Eastern
C.	Large	H.	Harbor
D.	Small	I.	Snow
E.	Western	J.	Water

Note

Allow students to create and argue for the definitions they employ when applying the classifications. For example, *large* might be interpreted as having "the population of Los Angeles," or "larger than the population of the city in which we live." Another student might take *large* to mean "a place of large farms," or "a place in which there are large (that is, heavy) amounts of snowfall."

Students can argue for their definitions and resultant applications during the class discussion of the activity.

24 Grouping Interest Center

Activity 23 can form the nucleus for an interest center. Students can work independently to combine the topic and classification items and then research and present supportive evidence concerning the validity of each combination.

25 The Match Game

Convert Activity 23 into the *Match Game.*

Use 3″ × 5″ index cards and make multiple copies of the topics and categories. Randomly distribute four topic cards to each player. Place all category cards into a box. Draw and announce one category card and then recognize the first three players who think they have a valid fit between the classification and one of their topic cards. Ask the first person with a hand in the air to give a brief statement of support for his or her particular match. If the response is plausible, then retrieve the topic card from the player. Then call on the second player, and then the third player. Players can have the same topic–classification match, but must offer supportive reasons not already offered during a particular round of play. The first person to lose all cards is declared the winner.

26 Categorizing List Items

Anytime a list of items is generated, consider asking the students to think of categories for those items. For example, let us say that you have asked the class to brainstorm various modes of transportation. The following list is developed:

Horse   Foot
Jet   Bike

18   SECTION 1

>   Rocket   Roller skates
>   Sailboat   Train
>   Car

Now ask the students to think of classifications for these transportation modes. One group of students came up with the following classifications:

>   Exercise
>   Fast
>   Fuel
>   Engine
>   Low-cost
>   Recreation
>   Wheels
>   Natural power

✤ 27 *Multiple Classifications*

To help the students understand the notion of multiple classification possibilities, ask them to determine all of the classifications that are applicable to each transportation mode.

Example: (refer to Activity 26)

>   Horse: exercise, fast, recreation, natural power
>   Jet: fast, fuel, recreation, wheels

✤ 28 *Name Categories*

Distribute a list of all the names of individuals in the class. Have the students think of classifications for the names (such as begin with a *C, R,* etc.; four letters; etc., names of a month; names of a celebrity; names of parents).

29 Simultaneous Categorizing

This activity has the positive attribute of involving everyone simultaneously.

Generate a list of phenomena around any topic (such as things needed to build a house). Distribute 3" × 5" index cards and have each student enter on separate cards each of the listed phenomena. Then distribute three additional index cards and have each student create three categories that fit the phenomena. The final step is to have the students arrange the phenomena under their category cards. Consider having students work in cooperative pairs for this activity.

30 Box Categories

Fill a box with a variety of items such as the following:

Hair brush	Repair manual
Comb	Magazine
Sponge	Newspaper
Rag	Pencil
Cup	Telephone book
Plate	Eye glasses
Eating utensils	Bar of soap
Oil can	TV program directory
Wrench	Bottle of vitamins
Cook book	

Ask groups of students to select and display the appropriate items for such classifications as:

        Kitchen
        Cleaning

Repairing
Garage
Relaxing
etc.

See Figure 30.

Figure 30

☼ 31 *Category Detectives*

Use the same box of items mentioned in the description of Activity 30. However, ask a group of two or three students to scan the available items, privately to agree on one category, and then to display the appropriate items for their selected category. Then have other students look over the display and try to identify the category for which items were chosen.

☼ 32 *Classification Charades*

Draw a chalk circle of about five feet in diameter on the floor. Into a shoe box place a series of cards, each with a "personal characteristic" such as one of the following:

SKILLS 21

Black hair	Boys
Taller than me	Girls
Shorter than me	Left-handed
Blond hair	Wearing a belt
Brown eyes	Wearing braids
Blue eyes	Wearing braces

A team of five to eight students play the game together. One team member draws a personal characteristic card from the box and moves into the circle all members of the team who fit the classification. Team members not within the circle guess at the category exemplified. Except for making the guesses, no talking is allowed among team members. You might also want to impose a time limit of about two minutes.

Variations

Time how long it takes a team to guess the category. Also, consider allowing team members to pose questions to the students in the circle *if* the questions can be answered with a *yes* or *no* response.

As the game progresses, consider using multiple classifications (such as girls with blue eyes; blonds who are left-handed; dark hair and braces). It might be necessary to display a list of all the categories in order to keep the game moving along.

33 *Categories Grids*

A grid (Figure 33, p. 22) and related word list are distributed. Students use the word list to make appropriate entries in the various grids.

Word List

| Knife | Pencil |
| Boat | Newspaper |

22 SECTION 1

        Napkin   Record player
        Plate   TV
        Trash can   Baseball bat
        Table   Playing cards
        Tablets   Book
        Chalk tray   Desk

	Eating	Learning	Relaxing, resting
Paper			
Metal or plastic			
Wood			

Figure 33

34 *Learning Clusters*

As a way of summarizing a lesson (or of summarizing the activity of a morning, afternoon, day, or week), ask the students to brainstorm everything that has happened during that period of time. Then have them think of categories that describe the listed activities.

Variation

Supply categories such as the following:

              Listening
              Speaking
              Reading
              Writing
              Running
              Feeling

For each category ask for examples of activity that occurred during the period of time specified.

35 *Classifying the Classifieds*

From several sections of the classified ads of a newspaper, cut out ads and distribute to groups of two or three students. List the classifications used. Read each category and have students raise their hands if they think they have an appropriate ad.

36 *Stand-up Categories*

One way to get all students involved simultaneously with a categorizing activity is to have them stand up or raise a hand if a particular category "fits." For example, after having the students draw pictures of something "they really enjoy," ask them to stand up if their picture includes: (a) a game, (b) running, (c) sitting, (d) more than one person, etc. Also, ask them to suggest additional categories.

37 *Category Combinations*

List two sets of descriptors on the board, like those listed below.

List A (activity-function)	List B (colors)
Cleaning	Red
Writing	Yellow
Moving	Blue
Sitting	Orange
Protecting	Green
Supporting	Black
Holding	Brown

24   SECTION 1

Have students form a category by combining one entry from List A with one from List B and indicating an item that fits the resultant category.

Examples

writing (A), yellow (B):	pencil
cleaning (A), brown (B):	broom
protecting (A), green (B):	shirt

Variation

Add a third list, List "C" Shape and feel: square, round, hard, soft, brittle, etc.

38   *Categories Grids*

On the classroom floor, make a *categories grid,* using different colors of plastic tape. The different colored *X*'s allow a quick and easy identification of a particular square. The permanent nature of the grid is intentional, as it can be used frequently throughout the year. (See Figure 38, p. 25.)

Notice, for example, that Activity 30 could be modified and used here by assigning kitchen, cleaning, repairing, and garage to specific squares and by placing the items contained in the box accordingly.

Comparing/Relating

39   *Continuous Comparisons*

Anytime you have two objects, ideas, or responses, seek a comparison. For example, with any two pictures, you can ask for an identification of what can be seen (observing process) as well as how things are alike and different. Have the students compare how what is being read, observed, or learned in class is both alike and different from some-

SKILLS 25

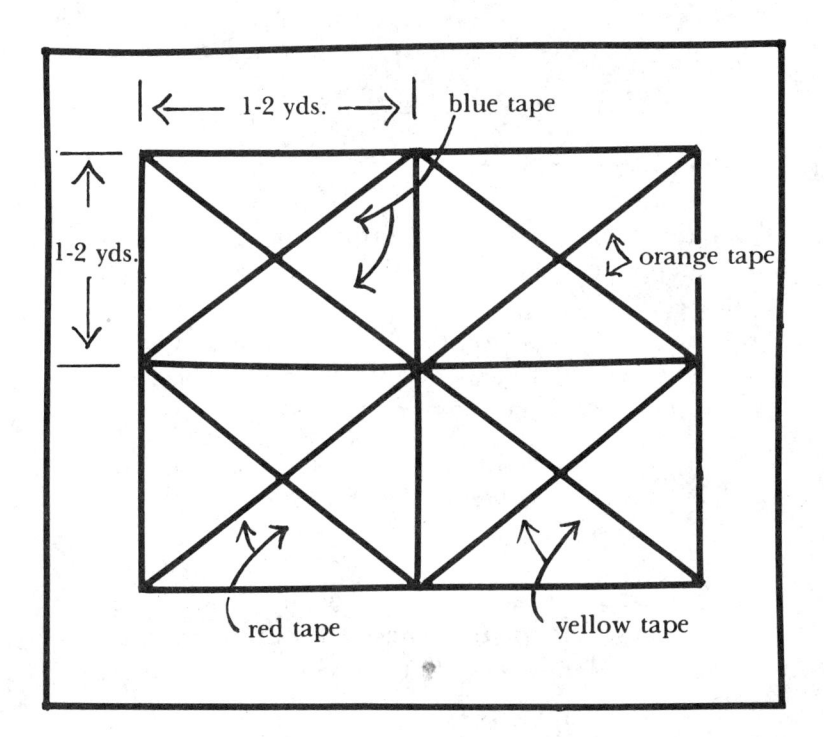

Figure 38

thing in today's world and how it relates to their own life experiences. Similarly, when several student responses have been given, consider asking a student to summarize how the statements are alike/different and with which one the student can best identify.

40 *Yellow Pages Comparisons*

Distribute the telephone Yellow Pages from two communities of varying size. Select one heading (such as Restaurants) and have the students compare the listings for the two communities (the number of restaurants, the types of restaurants). In determining and comparing the types of restaurants, it would probably be helpful first to list the restaurants under various classifications (fast food, French,

26 SECTION 1

Mexican, Italian; steak, etc.) and then to make comparative statements.

☼ 41 *Comparing Accounts*

Obtain two or more newspaper accounts of the same event. For example, you might get different accounts of the World Series, the Super Bowl, or even a highly publicized local event. Have the students compare the accounts in terms of factual data and of the kinds of explanations given and the conclusions drawn.

☼ 42 *Comparing Classrooms*

Have students visit a classroom different in grade level from theirs and compare their room with it. For example, compare the room size, the kinds of furniture and its arrangement, the kinds of books that are used, and the daily schedule.

Note

This activity requires using the "observing" process, ideas for which have been outlined in a previous section. See also Activity 7.

☼ 43 *Comparing Textbooks*

Involve students in a comparison of textbooks from varying grade levels (size of print, number of pages, size of pages, topics, etc.). Have the students offer reasons on why any differences exist.

☼ 44 *Comparing Ideas, Products*

Have students pair off to compare objects, ideas, products, etc.

SKILLS 27

Let us say that the students have completed drawings showing how their family divides the labor around the house (see Figures 44a, and 44b, p. 28). Rather than immediately sharing the pictures with the entire class, students could turn to the person next to them and discuss several things that are alike as well as different about their pictures. This activity can be followed by asking the members of each pair to summarize publicly what similarities and differences were discussed.

Variation

Randomly assign students to discussion-pairs. Ask them to discuss what is alike and different about their ideas, feelings, or products they have created.

Figure 44a

28 SECTION 1

Figure 44b

45 Red-Green Procedure

A red card and a green card are distributed to each student. The procedure can be used whenever the potential for a "yes-no," "agree-disagree" situation exists. For example, you might ask if women in the military, like men, should participate in combat situations. Allow the students some time (about one to two minutes) to think silently about the question. Then, at your signal, ask the students to hold up one of the cards: green to show agreement with the statement and red to indicate disagreement. Ask the students to hold up their selected card, find someone with a different colored card, and then compare their differences of opinion. An alternate, of course, is to have students locate others with similar choices and compare the reasons behind their responses.

46 Interest Center for Comparing

Set up an interest center displaying two pictures, items, ideas, etc., that involves students in comparing phenomena (see Figure 46).

There are several ways to involve the students in the interest center and to check their results:

1. Tape record the instructions. On another tape recorder have students record their responses and turn in the cassette for evaluation.
2. Have a student monitor the interest center, provide assistance to others when needed, and possibly even evaluate the results.

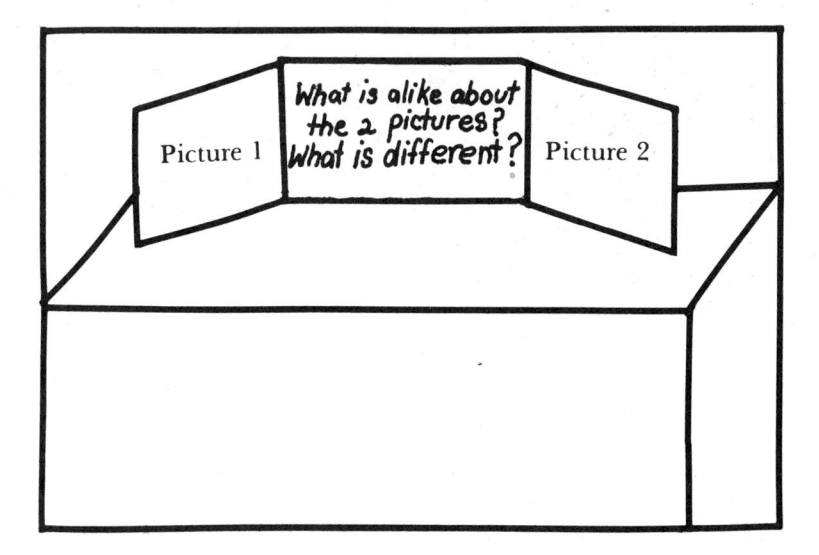

Figure 46

3. Use a coversheet that programs the reader through the experience.

Suggestions

In advance, record as many possible responses as you can think of for each of the displays. Have students compare this evaluation cassette with their own efforts. Invite participating students to add to those responses found on the evaluation tape.

Each week, involve selected students in changing the displays, creating new evaluation tapes, and monitoring their interest center.

47 *Relationship Mobiles*

On a piece of tag-board write the name of a person, event, concept, or topic that has been studied. This is the root card. Using tag board or index cards, write a series of words or phrases (facts, "other" concepts, ideas, names, etc.) that can be associated with the content of the root card. These are relationship cards. Cut strips of string of about 6" each and to each end tie a small clamp. The number of relationship cards indicates how many string-clamp set ups you will need. Attach the root card to a ceiling fixture. Display the relationship cards along a chalk tray. Students add to the mobile by selecting a relationship card, indicating the connection to the root card, and using the string-clamps to make the physical connection. See Figure 47.

Notice that the relationship cards could be used as root cards for other mobiles.

Alternative

Instead of constructing a mobile, glue a strip of sandpaper to the back of each card and use a flannel board for lining up the cards.

SKILLS 31

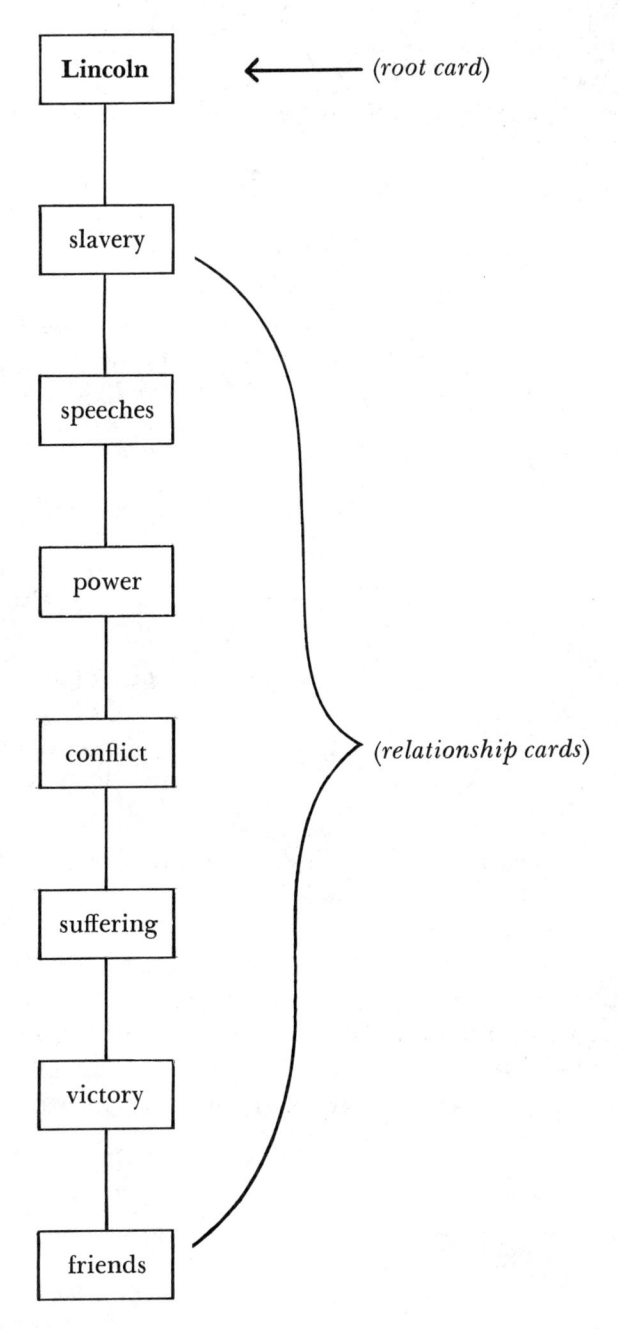

```
Lincoln  ←——— (root card)
   |
slavery ⎫
   |    ⎪
speeches⎪
   |    ⎪
 power  ⎪
   |    ⎬ (relationship cards)
conflict⎪
   |    ⎪
suffering⎪
   |    ⎪
 victory⎪
   |    ⎪
 friends⎭
```

Figure 47

✱ 48 *Relating Events*

Write a 5″ × 8″ card for a series of items within a category.

Example:

Category: Events

Items
- Columbus discovers America
- Landing the first humans on the moon
- Lindbergh's solo flight across the Atlantic
- Sputnik
- The Concorde lands for the first time in the United States

Items
- John Glenn's flight into space
- Breaking the land speed record at the Bonneville Salt Flats in Utah
- Completing the first Pony Express ride
- The first human beings take up residence in a space station (*future*)

Place the cards, back side showing, along a chalk tray. A student selects any two cards and indicates how the two events are (were, might be) alike and different in terms of the characteristics, circumstances, consequences, implications, etc. The topics can flow from what you have been studying and can be as simple as "animals," "places in the neighborhood," or, "people I know." For low level or nonreaders, substitute pictures for the written cards.

✱ 49 *Relating the Current with the Historical*

Each week, select one current event and locate a comparable event in history.

50 Relating the Historical with the Personal

Have students relate historical events to what has occurred during their own life.

Example

1. Are there any present-day Boston Tea Parties?
2. How was the California Gold Rush like the building of the Alaskan pipeline? How was it different?
3. How was the life of an eight-year-old living in colonial America like/different from your life today?
4. What are some of the things you do with your time that your parents also did when they were your age? What is different?

51 Circle Relationships

Display various objects (such as a thimble, glass, bottle, thread, milk carton, pencil, ball point pen) on a table. Use a length of yarn of about 24" to form a circle. Ask students to place the two objects that are most alike (most different, go best together, etc.) within the circle and then to give reasons for their choices. See Figure 51, p. 34.

Note

The criteria used to make the selections will probably vary among the students. For example, "most alike" for one student might be determined on the basis of size, but for another, on the basis of function.

Variation

Ask a student to look at the selections made by another student and then to attempt to determine what criteria were used.

Figure 51

❂ 52 *Simultaneous Relating*

In this activity, all students are involved simultaneously in a relating activity. Use the floor setup described in Activity 38, and place an object in each square.

Give each student a strip of paper (about 2" × 4") for each color represented by the squares. Ask the students to select the two squares that have objects that go best together (are most alike) and to place on their desk tops the paper strips that show the corresponding squares. After all students have indicated their selections, ask individuals to indicate their choices and reasons. Many responses should be anticipated and encouraged, since the choice of criteria will control the selections made.

SKILLS   35

Figure 52

Variation

Occasionally have students indicate their vote by holding up their selected colored strips. Call on students to attempt to explain the reasoning behind the selections made by their colleagues.

☼ 53 *Relationship Cards*

Form two lists of topics (concepts, personalities, cities, products, etc.) that have been studied.

Example

        List I   **List II**

1. Role   A. Family
2. Norms   B. Church

36   SECTION 1

  3. Change   C. Our classroom
  4. Learning   D. Cub Scouts, Brownies
  5. Division of labor   E. Baseball team
  6. Status

Write the number or letter designated for each item on a card and place it in two shoe boxes (one for each list). Have a student draw one card from each box and then describe a relationship between the two selected items (for example, the relationship between division of labor, List I, and family, List II).

54 *What Is Behind a Name?*

Make a list of first names for:

    Everyone in the class
    Parents' names
    Grandparents' names

Have the students compare the three lists: Which names are on all of the lists? Which ones are only on the list for our class? Which names are/were most popular? What are some possible reasons for these observations?

Follow-up

Students can discuss with their parents how their name was chosen and share this information with the class.

Predicting/Hypothesizing/Educated Guessing

55 *What Is Taking Shape?*

Have students predict what new construction in the neighborhood is going to be and offer supportive evidence (shape of what has already been constructed, comparison to surrounding phenomena, etc.). Allow individuals to change their guesses as construction develops.

Suggestion

Take pictures of the construction site as it is developing. Under each picture, list several of the predictions with the names of the students making a specific prediction.

56 *Predicting What Is Next*

Interrupt a record, film, or reading before its completion and ask the students to predict the next sequence, conclusion, statement of fact, word identification, problem, etc., that will follow.

57 *Field Trip Prediction Grids*

Students can predict what they will see on a field trip. Have the students brainstorm everything that comes into their mind as they anticipate what they will see during the field trip. List their ideas on the board. Then involve the class in predicting the salient characteristics of several of the objects.

For example, a class took a field trip to an open school. Their school was fairly traditional (fixed curriculum, one teacher for all subject areas, almost all of the instruction carried out in one classroom). The students knew that the open school was housed in an old warehouse that had been refurbished by staff, students, and parents. Some of their predictions are listed here:

(A) What we will see	(B) How it (they) will appear	(C) What was observed
Teachers	Like ours—but dressed differently	

(A) What we will see	(B) How it (they) will appear	(C) What was observed
Kids	Look like us—but noisier, and maybe not paying attention, not too friendly	
Classrooms	Not as bright as ours, kids wandering around not doing anything, desks and chairs for each student	
Books, maps, globes, paper	Arranged like ours	
Halls	Yellow, light green, some pictures hanging on them; sometimes what is hanging up will be student work	
	Students running, pushing, shoving	
Floors	No carpeting, concrete, wood sometimes	
Playground	Small, no slides, no bars, no jungle gyms	
Cafeteria	Serving trays, food like ours (sometimes good, sometimes bad) yellow walls, long tables with attached benches	
Principal	Man, younger than ours, friendly, wearing a suit but no tie	
Auditorium	Probably do not have one yet.	

Notice that a column (C) had been left blank so that the students could record what was observed and later compare it to their predictions (A), (B). The lists as shown could be duplicated and used as an observation guide during the field trip or as a summary guide afterwards. Also, as an alternative to having individuals write down observations, groups of students could work cooperatively and tape record their observations.

58 *Predicting Before Studying*

Involve students in making predictions about places, persons, and things they are about to study.

Example 1

The major population centers of Japan are going to be studied. An overlay of an outline of Japan's main islands is projected onto the chalk board. Students take turns predicting where Japan's largest cities are located, by writing their initials on the chalk board within the projected map. Reference is then made to wall maps and books in order to check the guesses.[1]

Example 2

A study of the distribution of products, people, and natural resources within the United States is going to be studied. Outline maps of the United States are distributed before the study. Students are asked to do the following:

1. Write *H's* where three of the busiest harbors are probably located
2. Write an *F* in four states you think have mostly flat ground
3. Write an *S* in two states that have a lot of snow
4. Write *B* for baseball in four places that you think might have major league baseball teams.

1. Adapted from Ryan, Frank L. *Exemplars for the New Social Studies.* Englewood Cliffs, N.J.: Prentice-Hall, Inc., 1971, pp. 23–24.

59 *The Data Connection*

When implementing the previous two ideas, provide an opportunity for the students to indicate what additional data they would find helpful, and why, in responding to the activity.

60 *Predicting From Want Ads*

The following idea can be implemented if you have access to out-of-town newspapers.

Mask or cut out any indication in the want ads section of where the newspaper is from and distribute to the students. Also distribute the want ads from the local newspaper. Using any clues they can generate from the two sources, the students are to predict if the 'mystery' city is larger or smaller than their city and whether or not the two cities are located in the same state.

61 *Using Hypothetical Maps*

Create hypothetical maps and have students guess at 'best' locations for various phenomena. See Figure 61, p. 41.

Example

1. Where would be the best location for a new Disneyland-type amusement center?
2. What additional data would you also want to make such a guess? How would you go about it?

62 *Predicting Function*

Bring in a tool that is probably unfamiliar to the students. Ask them to guess at the intended use of the tool. By examining the features of the tool, the students should be able to offer data support for their guesses.

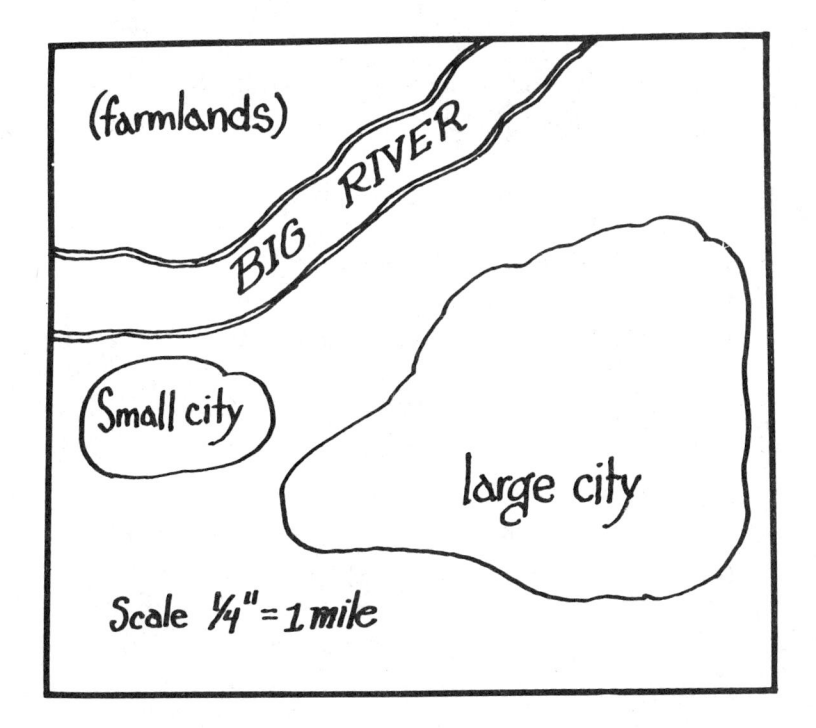

Figure 61

☼ 63 **What Will Happen?**

Over a period of several days, log observations of everyday phenomena: weather, things done in school, success of athletic teams, etc. Referring to the logs, predict the weather, how certain events will turn out at school, the scores of upcoming athletic contests, and any other event that might be predicted from the data that have been collected.

☼ 64 **"What Would Happen If . . .?" Questions**

Punctuate lessons with "What would happen if . . .?" questions that allow students to guess and imagine the consequences of a particular situation.

42   SECTION 1

Examples

>What would happen if animals could talk?
>What would happen if students did not have to attend school?
>What would happen if we had to get along without electricity?
>What would happen if you were principal of the school?
>What would happen if we had universal peace?
>What would happen if electric pencils were available?

65 *Time Circles*

Use time circles to help organize the students' predictions for a "What would happen if . . .?" question (Activity 64).

Draw three concentric circles on the board and have the students indicate when their prediction would take place. List the prediction on the appropriate circle. See Figure 65.

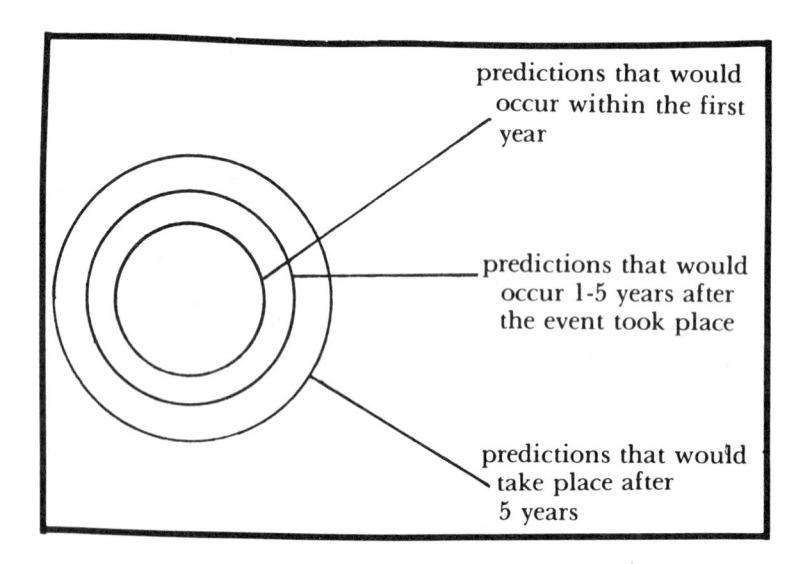

- predictions that would occur within the first year
- predictions that would occur 1-5 years after the event took place
- predictions that would take place after 5 years

Figure 65

Alternative 1

After brainstorming predictions, distribute copies of the concentric circles and have students individually indicate the appropriate locations.

Alternative 2

Use oak tag to make a chart showing the time circles. Enter the predictions on separate oak-tag strips. Display the chart on a bulletin board and have individuals pin the strip with the predictions to the appropriate time circle. Invite discussion of the various placements.

66 Prediction Chains

Involve the students in forming prediction chains in which relationships among predictions are indicated.

Example

What would happen if an automatic pencil were invented?

Responses:

Would need help in learning how to use it
We would use it in the schools
People would wonder what it was—maybe not like it
No more wooden pencils
Confusion
Need classes in how to use it

Possible Chain

Confusion ------ Need help in learning ------ Taught
               how to use it   how to
What is it?   use it:

　　　　　　　　　　　　　　　Use it in schools

　　　　　　　　　　　　　　　No more wooden pencils
　　　　　　　　　　　　　　　(i.e., conventional)

✦ 67 Re-Examining the Initial Prediction

By setting up *Prediction Chains,* (Activity 66), students sometimes question their initial predictions.
　　For example:

Would an automatic pencil mean the end to a need for wooden pencils?

Would anyone learn how to use the automatic pencil?

Would everyone who learned how to use the automatic pencil continue to use it instead of the more conventional pencil?

✦ 68 Adding Linkages to a Prediction Chain

An embellishment of the *Prediction Chain* (Activity 66) is to create branches to the main chain.

Example

What Would Happen If We Had An Automatic Pencil?
Confusion ------ Learn how to use it ------ Use the automatic pencil

　　Not learn how　　Not use the
　　to use it　　　　automatic ------ Use "regular"
　　　　　　　　　　pencil　　　　　　pencils

　　　　Use "regular"
　　　　pencils

✦ 69 Self-Selecting

Ask the students to consider the possibility that a new structure (such as a fast-food franchise, a grocery store, an ice cream store) is going to be built in their community. Where would be the best site for this new structure? Why?

Suggestion

Conduct field studies to collect data for a site selection.

70 *Hypothetical Situations*

Dealing with the following hypothetical situations would be especially appropriate for students studying, or with a background in, various geographical features, including population distribution, within the United States.

Question for Discussion

Where would be the best site in the United States (or, in our state) for each of the following:

1. The summer Olympics
2. The winter Olympics
3. The Super Bowl
4. The World Series
5. The World's Fair
6. The (Democratic, Republication) national convention
7. A new Disney-like amusement center

Allow sufficient opportunity for students to gather and offer support for their proposals.

Displaying Predictions

The following activities (71–74) for displaying predictions are especially helpful when such predictions are used as research hypotheses to be tested by the students. A later section of this chapter discusses various activities for involving students in classroom research.

☼ 71 *Hypotheses Display*

Ditto off pictures of choices and distribute a copy to each student. See Figure 71a.

Example

Question: Who can run faster, boys or girls?
Display a 3′ × 6′ strip of butcher paper. Students pin (paste, tape) choices on appropriate section of area A. Area B could be used to display any resultant data. See Figure 71b, p. 46.

With this display the hypotheses are quickly processed. Also, the display can be quickly taken down and stored until the lesson is to continue.

Figure 71a

SKILLS 47

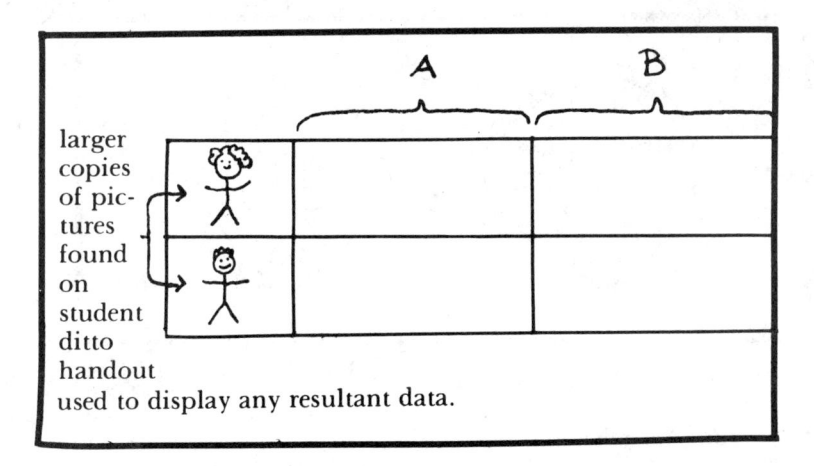

[A | B table with stick figures of a girl and a boy in the left column]

larger copies of pictures found on student ditto handout used to display any resultant data.

Figure 71b

☼ **72 Red-Green Display**

When a prediction is being made between two alternatives, the red-green card procedure as outlined in Activity 45 is applicable. For example, in the previous activity, green could represent girls, and red, boys. On cue from the teacher, students could simultaneously hold up a green or red card to indicate their prediction of whether boys or girls run faster.

☼ **73 Penny History**

Display a penny. Have the students imagine where the particular penny has been. See Figure 73.

Possible questions

What do we know for sure about the coin? (when it was "born," that it has been in our classroom, whether it is older or younger than us).
Do you think it has ever traveled out of our city? Out of our state? Out of our country? Why? How might you be able to keep track of where a coin has been?

Figure 73

74 *Pocket Chart*

Create a pocket chart for displaying individual student predictions, using 8″ × 11″ clasp-type envelopes and tag board. See Figure 74.

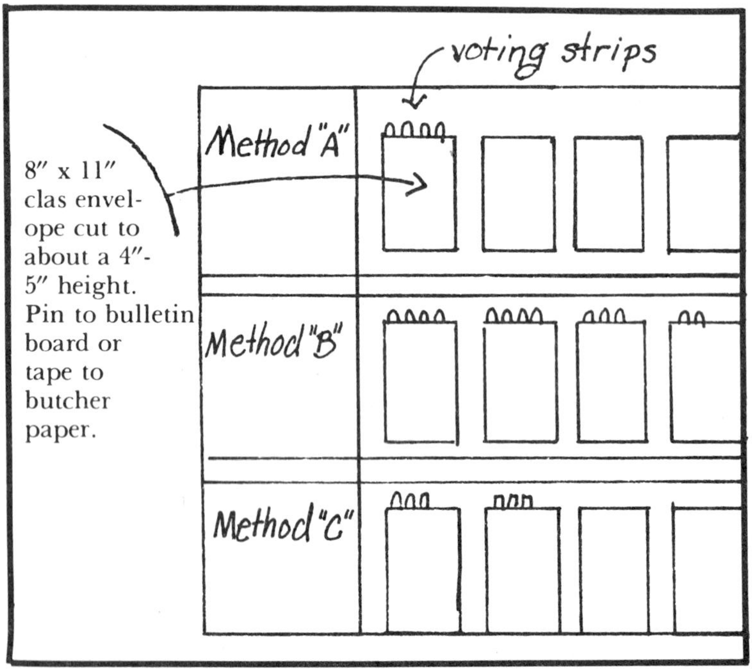

Figure 74

Problem

What is the best way to study spelling—Method A? Method B? or Method C?

Issue to each student a voting strip (about a 1½" × 6" strip of colored tag board or construction paper). Students place their voting strip in the envelope opposite their predictive choices.

Inferring

75 *"Things I Like To Do" Checklist*

Ask the students to complete a "Things I Like to Do" checklist like the one shown below (ten to fifteen items from those listed are probably ample).

Checklist of Things I Like To Do

Directions: Look over the things listed. Check the five things you like to do the most

_____ Read
_____ Listen to music
_____ Sing
_____ Listen to the radio
_____ Look at TV
_____ Play a musical instrument
_____ Stay over night at someone else's house
_____ Swim
_____ Talk to other children
_____ Talk to adults
_____ Play baseball
_____ Play basketball
_____ Play soccer
_____ Play football
_____ Play _____ (fill in with something you like, but that is

50   SECTION 1

                                    not found anywhere on this list)

_____ Go to school
_____ Do something with a parent
_____ Go to movies
_____ Babysit
_____ Collect stamps
_____ Take care of a pet
_____ Math
_____ Social studies
_____ Write stories
_____ Go camping
_____ Go fishing

Description:

Then have the students fold their completed checklist and place and seal it in a blank envelope. Mix up all of the envelopes and randomly redistribute them to the students. Have the students use the space at the bottom of the questionnaire to write two to four sentences that describe the person represented by the responses on the checklist. Ask for volunteers to share what they have written.

Possible focus questions

1. How is the person you just described like you? Different from you? How do you know?
2. Is the person you described a boy or a girl? What are your reasons for what you say?
3. Do you think the person you described would be interested in any of the following? Why or why not?
   a. Entering the school's science fair?

b. Learning about rocks and rock collecting?
c. Being in a classroom (school) talent show?
d. Jogging?
e. Writing a play and presenting it to others in the class?
f. Showing visitors around the school?

76 *The Incident*

Stage a short (ten to forty-five second) incident in class. For example, you might have another teacher enter your room carrying a shoe box. While talking to you, the shoe box slips to the floor and 'something' (such as a chalkboard eraser, a handful of pencils, a play snake or lizard) drops out. After a brief scurry the 'something' is placed back in the box and the teacher leaves the room.

Possible followup activities

1. Ask three to four volunteers to go separately to another classroom and describe the incident. Then have three to four students from that classroom go to the classroom in which the incident took place and describe what happened. Students who witnessed the incident can compare their perceptions with those who reported.
2. Immediately after the incident, have students brainstorm everything they observed. List the observations and discuss any discrepant observations.
3. Individually tape record eye-witness accounts of three or so observers of the incident. Play each tape back to the class. Possible focus questions:
   1. How are the tapes alike? How are they different?
   2. In your opinion which are the best? Why?

77 *Picture Communication*

Ask each student to fold a sheet of drawing paper into thirds. The student is then to use the thirds to draw sim-

52   SECTION 1

Figure 77

ple pictures to show his or her activity from the time school got out until going to bed that evening. See Figure 77. The pictures are then exchanged and volunteers are asked to describe the activity of a classmate using the artist's rendition as a data source.

78   *Data Boxes*

Have students select artifacts from one room at home that will fit into a shoe box. The *Data Boxes* are exchanged at school and others use the contents to infer what room is represented. See Figure 78.

79   *Textbook Inferences*

Locate examples of inferences made in social studies textbooks. Involve students in a determination of what data

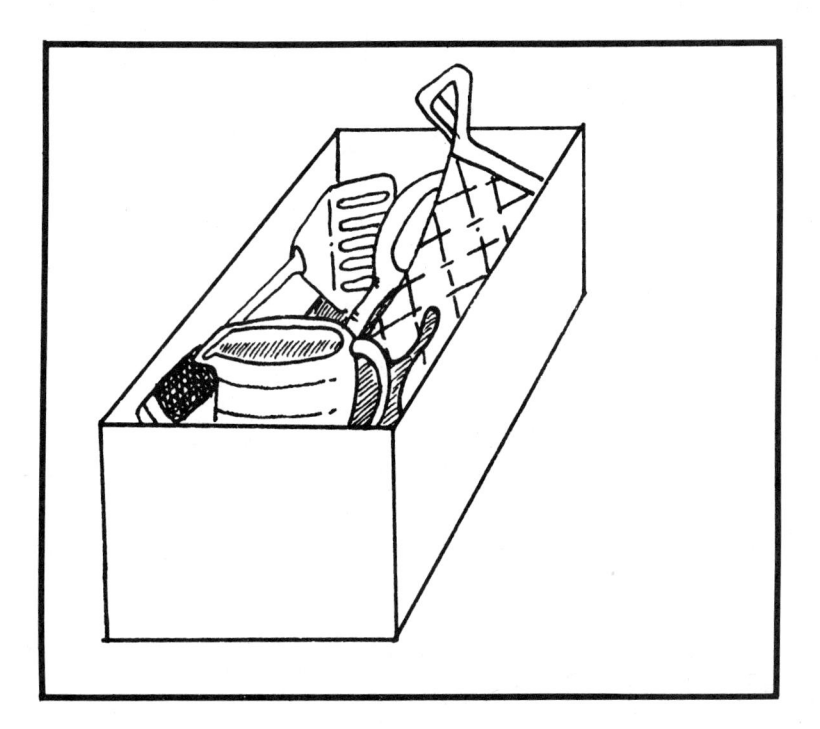

Figure 78

are required to support the inferences. Consider the following selection:

Life in a Mexican Village *

Village people work very hard for very little money. But they are cheerful and friendly and always ready to share what they have. They love their children and want big families, even if it means sacrifice and more work. Their life is hard, but they have love and religious faith. So they are usually happy, and life is good.

Focus questions

  1. What are the inferences?

---

* *Mexico*, by P. A. Ross, The Fideler Company, Grand Rapids, Michigan, 1967, p. 100.

54 SECTION 1

2. What kinds of data would have to be gathered in order to conclude that village people are happy people, etc.?
3. What are some ways of collecting these data?
4. In your opinion does the author have enough evidence to make these inferences? What are your reasons?

80 *Interpreting the Poll*

Present only the data results of a national poll and provide space for the students to draw their own inferences. Consider the varied interpretations given and then compare to the interpretations given by the pollster. Ask individuals to agree or disagree with the inferences offered by others.

81 *Data Retrieval Charts*

To guide students in collecting data from a reading, discussion, film, interview, or lecture, provide several categories around which the data can be collected and organized. An example of a retrieval chart used to record data from various student readings on transportation is shown in Figure 81.

After the data retrieval is accomplished, the stage is set for inferring (and other process) activity, through such questions as the following:

1. Use the two lists of data to compare the comfort of transportation modes for the years indicated. (Additional comparisons could focus on: speed, danger, cost.)
2. Using the two lists, describe what changes in transportation have taken place over the years. What inventions were needed for these changes to take place?
3. What are some kinds of travel that might be included in a list for the year 2000?

SKILLS 55

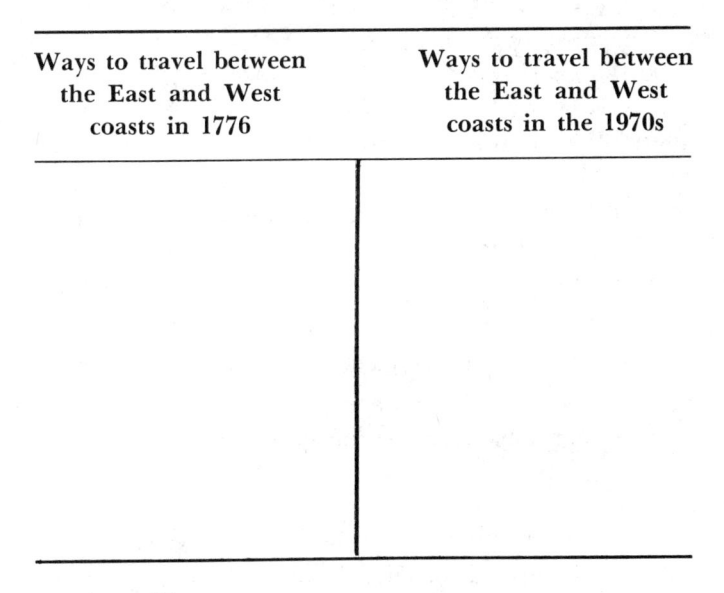

Ways to travel between the East and West coasts in 1776	Ways to travel between the East and West coasts in the 1970s

Figure 81

82 Data Retrieval Charts and Student Reports

Data Retrieval charts are also an excellent device for elevating the low-level thinking that frequently accompanies student presentation of reports. For example, students may be operating in committees to gather data on the main natural resources of various countries. Major resources for each country could be listed and displayed on a bulletin board.

Questions like the following might then be employed:

1. Which countries have some of the same natural resources?
2. Which countries could help one another in terms of natural resources?
3. With which countries would the United States probably be most interested in trading resources? Why?

83 Selecting Appropriate Inferences

Sometimes students recognize appropriate inferences for various sets of data, but experience great difficulty in creating the inferences. Consider offering several possible inferences for a set of data and having the students argue for the most appropriate ones.

For example, the following inferences might be presented as possible interpretation for data collected on modes of transportation for the years 1776 and 1977:

1. Travel was more interesting in 1776.
2. People enjoyed traveling more in 1776.
3. Travel is less dangerous than it used to be.
4. There are now more ways to travel across the United States than there were 200 years ago.
5. Travel costs have gone up.
6. Travel can be faster than it was 200 years ago.

For those inferences considered inappropriate by the students, ask them to describe what additional data would need to be collected in order to give support to the statement.

84 Inference Scenario

Create a brief scenario and several related inferences. Ask the students to choose and argue for the best inferences, offering data support for their choices. Several examples follow.

Scenario A

Don was asked by his mother to go to the store to buy laundry soap. He left for the store an hour ago, but has not yet returned home.

Inferences to consider for Scenario A:

1. Don is lost.
2. Don's mother will call the police.
3. Don's mother is worried.
4. Don lives out in the country.
5. Don might be in trouble.
6. The store is a long distance from home.
7. Don is old enough to go to the store by himself.
8. Don forgot what he was supposed to do.
9. Things are very busy at the store.

Scenario B

Ann called Clara to invite her over to play on Thursday. However, the girls did not play.

Inferences to consider for Scenario B:

1. Ann and Clara know each other.
2. Ann and Clara are friends.
3. One of the girls is mad at the other.
4. The girls probably got together on another day.
5. Clara was busy and could not play.
6. Ann probably got mad at Clara for not coming over.
7. Ann was upset that Clara could not play on Thursday afternoon.

85 *Inference Analysis Guide*

When involving students in an analysis of inferences, as in the case with the Inference Scenario, Activity 84, consider using an Inference Analysis Guide, such as the one shown in Figure 85, p. 58.

	True	Maybe True—Need More Data	Not True
Inference 1: Don is lost.			
Inference 2: Don's mother will call police.			
Inference 3: Don's mother is worried.			
Inference 4: (Etc.)			

Other inferences that can be made from the scenario:

_____

_____

_____

Figure 85

✽ 86 *Classroom Museum*

Students can collect their own artifacts and set up a museum in their classroom. However, choose museum topics taken from their own lives. See Figure 86, p. 59.

Examples

Toys, dolls, baseball, soccer, skateboarding, TV, music, surfing.

For each museum display, have someone explain what it 'tells' about today's children.

Figure 86

STUDENT RESEARCH

RATIONALE

Conducting research in the classroom can be an exciting activity that necessitates a multiple use of thinking processes. Students traditionally receive knowledge created by others, but seldom are personally involved in its generation. By varying the kinds of inquiry problems presented, as well as the amount of teacher direction, students at all levels of development can profit from personal involvement in research activity.

Research involvement should help the student further understand the nature of knowledge itself (its tentativeness, the necessity to cope with ambiguities, objectivity when reviewing evidence) as well as become more critical and analytical consumers of it.

The activities in this section should be considered in conjunction with those in a succeeding section that focus on the development of student skills in collecting original information.

Activities

87 TV Favorites

Create a list of seven or eight TV programs that you think your students enjoy. Have them guess which of the listed programs would be among the two favorites for class members. You could have the students indicate their guesses on a handout, which they sign and turn in. Then ask the students to discuss and give reasons for their choice. Tally the guesses and compare with the 'evidence' previously presented during the discussion period.

88 Extending 'TV Favorites'

Treat the guesses as hypotheses to be tested. Have the class discuss how the relevant data concerning program

SKILLS 61

preferences might be collected. After implementing the agreed on procedures, tally the results and compare to the original hypotheses.

89 *Using a Data Display Chart*

When conducting a research study such as described in Activity 87, it is helpful to create a *Data Display Chart* as the results evolve. See Figure 89.

Display a sheet of butcher paper, approximately 3′ × 6′. List the TV programs. Using small squares (1″ × 1″)

Favorite TV Programs of People in Our Class		
Hypotheses	TV Programs	Data
▫ ▫ ▫	Program 1	▫ ▫ ▫ ▫ ▫
▫ ▫	Program 2	▫ ▫
▫	Program 3	▫ ▫
▫ ▫ ▫ ▫ ▫ ▫ ▫	Program 4	▫ ▫ ▫ ▫ ▫ ▫ ▫
▫ ▫	Program 5	▫
▫ ▫ ▫ ▫	Program 6	▫ ▫
▫ ▫ ▫ ▫ ▫	Program 7	▫

Figure 89

of construction paper, have the students attach a square alongside their program choices (hypotheses section).

Hint

Have students write their initials on their square for later identification.[1]

Using paper squares of a color different from those used to indicate their hypotheses have the students indicate the results of the data collection on the right-hand side of the chart.

Referring to the resultant research chart, the students can compare their original hypotheses with the data results and make inferential statements from the data.[2]

Other Research Ideas

Additional questions, suitable for initiating student research activity, are described here in Activities 89–96.

90 *Classes*

What are the favorite classes/events of students?

91 *School Activities*

What are the favorite school-time activities?

92 *Sports*

What are the favorite sports of students for (a) playing and (b) watching?

---

1. Refer again to Activities 55–74 for additional suggestions for displaying predictions (hypotheses).
2. For a discussion of three levels of inferring, refer to: Ryan, Frank L., and Arthur K. Ellis. *Instructional Implications of Inquiry.* Englewood Cliffs, N.J.: Prentice-Hall, Inc., 1974, pp. 125–131.

93 *Person Attributes*

What are two attributes you like to see most in a person?

94 *Colors*

What are your favorite colors?

95 *Absenteeism*

What day(s) of the week do students tend to be absent from our classroom most often?

96 *Using a Rank-Order Mode of Research*

Notice how, with slight modifications, the open-ended survey problems presented thus far can be changed into problems requiring a rank-order mode of response.

Example:

Activity 90: What are the favorite classes/events of students?

Rank order: Place a *1* before the class you like most, a *2* after your next favorite, and so on:

_____ Social Studies
_____ Math
_____ Reading
_____ Creative writing

An advantage of rank order-type research, especially with younger, inexperienced researchers, is that a definite limit has been set on the kinds of data that are to be considered, thus making the results more manageable than might be the case with open-ended surveys.

64   SECTION 1

☼ 97 *Processing Rank-Order Data*

The following problem will be used as suggestions are presented for processing rank-order data.

Problem

Place a *1* before the thing you like to do most often, a *2* after your next favorite activity, etc.

Which of the following do you like to do most of the time?

1. Read a book
2. Watch TV
3. Play a game like (Old Maid, Flinch, Monopoly)
4. Play a game like (kickball, four-square, jacks, dodgeball, baseball, football).

A simplified procedure for processing the data is to add up the number of *1*s indicated for each of the four alternatives and disregard the other rankings.

A more complicated procedure is to total the rankings for each of the alternatives. For example, let us say that alternative #1: *Read a book,* received the following rankings from the students surveyed: 1, 3, 4, 2, 2, 4, 4, 3, 3, 1, 4, 3, 2, 4, 1, 2, 3, 4, 3, 2, 4, 4, 1, 3, 2, 4. The sum for the rankings for alternative #1 is 73. Similarly, the sum of the rankings would be determined for each of the three remaining alternatives. Low scores would indicate the 'more preferred' (somewhat analogous to golf scores).

Other Rank-Order Ideas

Besides modifying Activities 90–97 to a rank-order style, consider implementing the following rank-order possibilities (Activities 98–106).

The instructions, in each case, would be a modification of those used in the preceding example (Activity 97).

98 Color Rankings

What is your favorite color?

1. Pink
2. White
3. Orange
4. Purple

99 Characteristic Rankings

What do you like to see most in a friend?

1. Humor
2. Neat appearance
3. Intelligence
4. Friendliness

100 Ranking Historical Events

Which of the following was the most important event in our country's history?

1. Landing a man on the moon
2. Reestablishing contacts with China in the 1970s
3. Nixon's resignation
4. The wheat deal with Russia

101 Issues Ranking

What is most important as an issue in our society?

1. Woman's rights
2. School integration
3. Job training in schools
4. Poverty

☼ 102 *Personal Attributes Ranking*

What do you like most about yourself?

1. Intelligence
2. Appearance
3. Humor
4. Getting along with others
5. Leadership abilities

☼ 103 *Learnings Ranking*

What was the most exciting thing you learned in school last week?

1. [Topic #1]
2. [Topic #2]
3. [Topic #3]

☼ 104 *Foods Ranking*

Which foods do you like?

1. Potatoes
2. Carrots
3. Lettuce
4. Peas

☼ 105 *Music Rankings*

Rank-order the following musical selections.

1. [Title of selection #1]
2. [Title of selection #2]

3. [Title of selection #3]
4. [Title of selection #4]

106 Ranking TV Program Categories

What is your favorite kind of TV program?

1. Sports
2. Movies
3. Variety show
4. Game show
5. Soap opera
6. Situation comedy
7. Cartoons

Note

Not all of these categories would have to be used. Also, consider the possibility of having students hypothesize toward the rank-order preferences of older/younger students and then collect, process, and infer from the relevant data.

107 Experimental Research in the Classroom

For each of the preceding ideas for conducting classroom research, data are collected that already exist (although they still need to be extracted by the researcher). However, research problems can also be posed for which the relevant data do not currently exist. In such situations, the researcher must identify and control the conditions of varied environments (that is, manipulate the key variables) in order to generate the appropriate data. Such research is typically called experimental research.

Again, as stated in the introduction to this section on

68 SECTION 1

classroom research, this author believes that with the appropriate instructional modifications, students at all levels of development can profit from an involvement with experimental research.

For example, you might ask the students to predict which of the following treatments would be most effective in learning an identical fifteen-word spelling list.

Treatment 1

Students are issued the spelling list and study it on their own for twenty minutes a day, for three successive days.

Treatment 2

The teacher writes one of the spelling words on the board. Working in unison, the students pronounce the word and spell it aloud. Then, individually and without looking at the board, each student writes the word. A comparison is then made between the word as just written and the spelling that is on the board. The concluding step is to make any necessary word corrections.

The preceding sequence of activity is repeated for each of the spelling words on the list over a period of twenty minutes a day for three successive days.

Treatment 3

Students write each word on the spelling list twenty times apiece, over a period of twenty minutes a day for three successive days.

108 *Using Tallies To Process Experimental Data*

In implementing the preceding research study (Activity 107), first have the students hypothesize (see previous suggestions for displaying predictions and setting up a data retrieval chart). Then, randomly assign the students to the three treatments, implement the treatments, and administer the spelling list as a final (i.e., post-) test. There are two ways to compare the results: (a) average the scores for each treatment, (b) tally the individual scores, as shown in Figure 108, p. 70.

Mode, Mean, Range

Other simple procedures that facilitate the drawing of comparisons between the treatments include finding the mean, the mode, and the range. In applying each of these procedures, data for the three spelling treatments presented in Activity 108 will be used.

109 *Mode*

The *mode* is the value that occurs most frequently in a distribution, just as the style of dress that occurs most frequently in a given season is called the *mode*.

	Treatment 1	Treatment 2	Treatment 3
Mode	14	17	16

Note

If adjacent intervals have the same frequency and it is larger than the frequency in other intervals, the mode is calculated to be at the midpoint of the entire range covered by these intervals.

110 *Mean*

The mean is determined by summing the scores for each treatment and then dividing by the number of scores.

SECTION 1

Number of words spelled correctly	Treatment 1	Treatment 2	Treatment 3
20	I	III	I
19	II	II	I
18	III	IIII	II
17	II	IIII	IIII
16	I	III	IIII II
15	I	II	III
14	IIII	II	I
13	I	II	I
12	I		I
11	I		I
10	I	I	II
9			
8	II		
7			
6	I		
5	I		
4			
3			
2			
1			

Figure 108

	Treatment 1	**Treatment 2**	**Treatment 3**
Scores:	Add: 20, 19, 19, 18, 18, 18, 17, 17, 16, 15, 14, 14, 14, 14, 14, 14, 13, 12, 12, 10, 9, 8, 8, 6, 5	20, 20, 20, 19, 19, 18, 18, 18, 18, 17, 17, 17, 17, 17, 17, 16, 16, 16, 15, 15, 14, 14, 13, 13, 10	20, 19, 18, 18, 17, 17, 17, 17, 17, 16, 16, 16, 16, 16, 16, 16, 15, 15, 15, 14, 13, 12, 11, 10, 10
Sum:	344	414	387
Total number of scores:	25	25	25
Mean = $\dfrac{\text{Sum of Scores}}{\text{Number of Scores}}$	13.76	16.56	15.48

111 *Range*

The *range* is the difference between the highest and lowest scores.

	Treatment 1	**Treatment 2**	**Treatment 3**
Range	5 — 20	13 — 20	7 — 20

On an examination of either the range, mode, mean, or by referring to all three collectively, one could say that Treatment 2 appears to have worked best as a group spelling strategy.

Notice how Activity 110 not only serves to involve students with the process of hypothesizing (as well as comparing and inferring) but also serves as a potential vehicle for gaining insight concerning the nature of school, teaching, and learning.

Other Experimental Research Ideas

Additional experimental research problems within which students can hypothesize, collect, process and relate data, and make inferences, are described in Activities 112–121.

112 *Push Ups*

Among three approaches, which is the best to increase the number of push ups?

113 *Speed*

Which of three training procedures is the best for improving running times in a 50/100 yard dash?

114 *Multiplication*

Which among three drill exercises is the best for learning multiplication tables?

115 *Rewards*

Which of three reward systems is most effective in our classroom?

Examples

Possible reward systems include:

1. Immediate reinforcement: material rewards (such as small prize, candy).

SKILLS 73

2. Delayed reinforcement: material rewards (such as give students tokens when a goal is attained, but redeem the tokens for a material reward at a later date).
3. Immediate reinforcement: nonmaterial rewards (such as verbal praise for a "good job," "good thinking," "well thought out response," etc., coming from the teacher, another adult, peers, or even self, at the time the "good" is being accomplished.
4. Delayed reinforcement: nonmaterial rewards (such as each Friday, set time aside for students to receive praise for their actions and accomplishments).

☸ 116 *Quick-Clean*

Which is the quickest of three student-suggested procedures for cleaning up the room after an involved art project?

Examples

1. Individual students clean up what they were using.
2. Tasks are identified and students volunteer for the task-related jobs.
3. A cleanup committee of five or six students cleans up the room while the remainder of the class goes on to a different activity.

☸ 117 *Centers of Attention*

Which of three kinds of interest centers attracts the most students?

Suggestion

Use identical content for each of the interest centers but vary the presentation modes:

1. Tape recordings
2. Readings

3. Tape recordings of a set of materials that the participant can follow.

118 *Seating Patterns*

Which of three classroom seating patterns is preferred by the students and is still acceptable to the teacher?
    Examples include:

Sitting next to a friend
Alternate boy-girl pattern—teacher assigned
Random assignment of students by the teacher

119 *Fire Drill*

Which of three traffic procedures is the fastest for evacuating the classroom during a fire drill?

120 *Best Sellers*

First collect data around the question: What kinds of books in the classroom library are chosen most frequently by the students? Then using the least popular titles, display the books in three different ways and determine which display, if any, increases book use.

121 *School—Lunch*

What is the relationship, if any, between living near the school and going home for lunch, bringing a lunch, and buying lunch in the cafeteria?

INFORMATIONAL SKILLS

RATIONALE

Although teacher intentions may be nobly conceived, frequently the development of informational skills is mistakenly thought of as an automatic by-product of having students faithfully reproduce paragraphs from one or two sources. The instructional shortcomings soon surface. Students are confused in trying to decide where to go for information, and copying becomes a substitute for personally organizing and processing the information. And finally, the report is turned in, or maybe worse, read to the class, resulting in the intellectual advancement of few, but the unrestricted boredom of many.

Needed is direct instructional attention to the multiple activities involved when using informational sources. The subtopics presented in this section (locating information; gathering and organizing information, including original information; processing information; and finally, alternatives for reporting) also constitute a sequence for helping students create order out of otherwise isolated pieces of data. Inclusion of the subtopic *Collecting Original Information* is in response to the notion that students can be directly involved in the generation of information and are not totally confined to what already exists in books, newspapers, and other data sources. Such a perspective is consistent with recent developments to involve students as inquirers as well as receivers of knowledge.

Locating Information

☼ 122 *Using Multiple Titles*

Hint

It is not unusual for there to be fewer than one copy of a specific social studies title available for each student. This is not a major obstacle to the development of student skills in locating information. Distribute the sources you do have on hand to pairs of students, who can take turns searching the different volumes for suitable information. As students exhaust these immediate sources, they can walk to other desks and borrow any other titles that are available. More able students can be given a free rein to browse anywhere in the room for appropriate sources and information.

123 *Headlining*

On separate tag-board strips, print several different headlines that reflect current events. Pin the headlines to the bulletin board, leaving space under each tag strip. Distribute newspapers that have been collected over several days. Students are to cut out articles and pin them to the space under the appropriate headings.

Note

As suggested in Activity 424, a particular news topic is focused on and reported. Implementing such a news emphasis approach is facilitated through Activity 123.

124 *Brainstorming Sources*

Hint

Before asking students to locate information on a topic, involve them in brainstorming all of the possible sources that might be helpful. Gather all suggested sources together and then assign the responsibility to individuals (or small groups of individuals) for checking specific items.

125 Newspapers As Information Sources

Collect newspapers for a period of several days (ask students to bring copies of newspapers as soon as they become available in their homes). Distribute a list of a series of specific informational items that can be found in the newspaper.

Examples might include:

The top four selling records
Where a specific movie is playing and the starting times
A score from a recent sporting event
The best deal on lettuce, hair spray, etc.
Sales jobs available

Students 'answer' the informational requests by cutting out the appropriate items, highlighting or underlining the specific information requested, and attaching it to the handout.

126 Narrowing the Focus

Hint

In having students look up information, begin with broad categories, which are easiest for locating sources, then move to categories that are increasingly specific. For example, rather than initially search for information on where wheat is grown in Canada, have the students locate all available references on Canada; then, on products in Canada; and finally, on wheat production in Canada.

127 The Wide-Angle Focus

Younger students can be involved in locating information. For example, let us suppose that the unit under study in-

78   SECTION 1

cludes an emphasis on travel. For a particular day, you might write on the board a simple direction such as:

> Find any information you can on cars.

Read and discuss this assignment. Review with the students the possible sources they might search and how pictures as well as words can give information. Allow some students to work together on their search. After the search period, allow as many students as possible to share the sources and information they located, including their interpretations of relevant photographs and illustrations.

※ **128   Reference Cards**

Older students can use 3″ × 5″ index cards to make simple reference cards like the one shown in Figure 128.

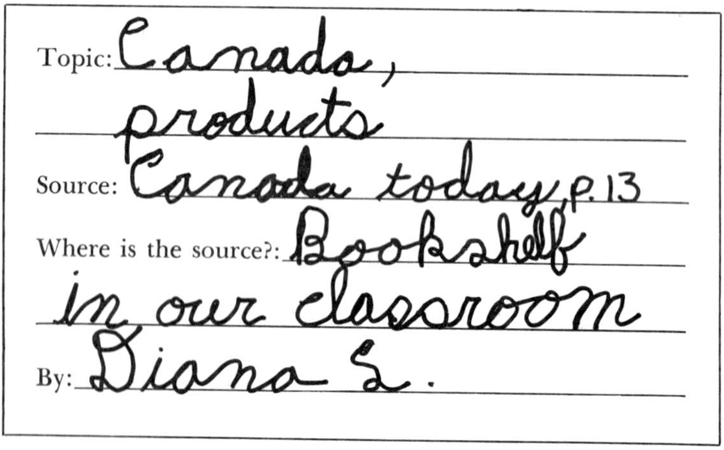

> Topic: Canada, products
> Source: Canada today, p. 13
> Where is the source?: Bookshelf in our classroom
> By: Diana S.

Figure 128

✤ 129 *Retrieval Envelopes*

On large mailing envelopes write a specific topic for which information is to be gathered. (See Figure 129.) As reference cards are completed, they can be deposited in the appropriate envelopes. This activity provides a good organizational base for follow-up activities involving retrieval and presentation of the information (refer to succeeding sections for suggested activities).

Alternative

If each student is to assume the responsibility for locating information on several topics, consider providing large letter envelopes to each student. An envelope can be used for each topic and the reference cards sorted accordingly.

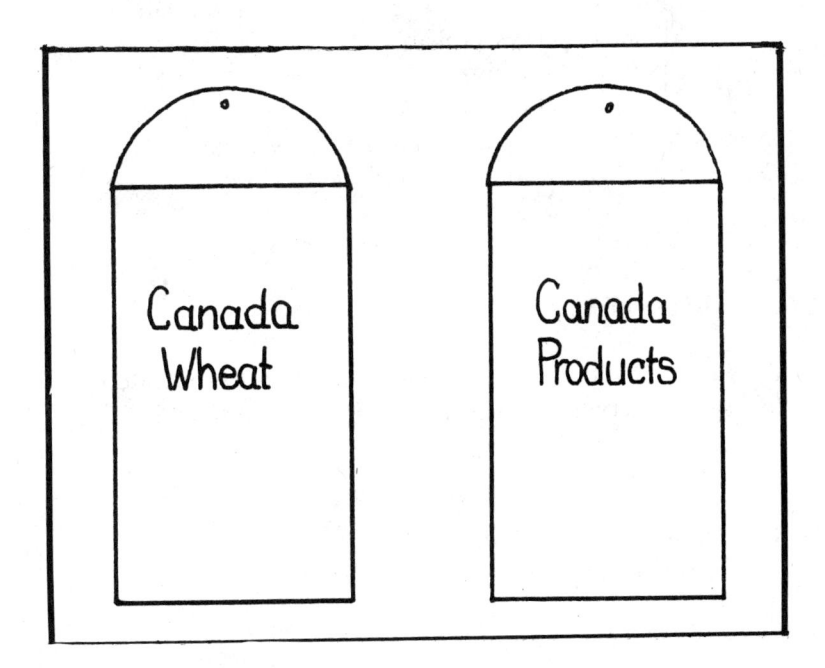

Figure 129

80   SECTION 1

☼ 130 *Today's Information for Tomorrow's Interpretation*

Alter the usual perspective for locating information through this activity. Set the stage for the activity by describing a situation like this:

> Your task is to create a set of references that will help someone twenty-five years from now understand what was happening in the United States [or, your particular state, or city] during this school year. The person will only have your reference cards available for doing this.

Suggested sequence of remaining procedures for implementing the activity:

1. Discuss what is the best information to include.
2. Discuss: What are the sources for such information? Will these sources probably be available twenty-five years from now? How can we check this?
3. Search for and cite the relevant references.
4. Select the best citations generated from (3).

Gathering and Organizing Information

☼ 131 *Bookmarking*

Provide blank bookmarks that can be used to indicate the location and type of data for a particular source. See Figure 131, p. 81.

☼ 132 *Students—Copying Machines*

Hint

Frequently we cast students in the role of copying machines under the pretense that copying word-for-word out

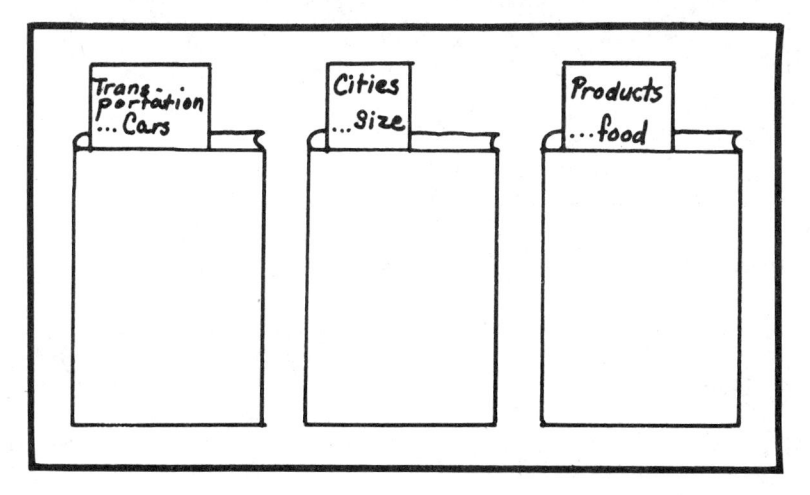

Figure 131

of a source is doing research. Discourage students from copying any source by hand before they have exhausted such alternatives as using a copying machine, using highlighter pens, or where possible, cutting out the relevant material.

※ 133 *Information Forms*

Duplicate and make available *Information Forms* that help students organize what is to be extracted from each source. Refer to an example of one possibility shown in Figure 133, p. 82.

※ 134 *Selling Your Sources*

When several sources are available on the same topic, occasionally have different students 'sell' the class on which source should be selected. Of course, this procedure does not rule out using several sources when gathering informa-

82 SECTION 1

Information Form

Source: _____

Topic: _____

Specific quotes needed: _____

_____

Specific facts needed: _____

_____

Main ideas needed: _____

_____

_____

Figure 133

tion, and it does contribute toward the development of student skills in deciding how to evaluate multiple sources.

135 *Information Sort*

When students have completed gathering information for a presentation, have them sort the various items into different groupings. Write a label for each grouping on an index card and clip to the items. Students can then arrange the groupings into the sequence to be used in their presentation. Also, within each grouping, students can sequence and number the order in which particular items might most effectively be used.

136 Guiding the Gathering

Hint

When you are having students work with several sources, provide short-answer, guiding questions that can only be answered by using more than one source.

Examples

> Using the two books handed out, write several sentences to describe what it is like to drive a car in downtown Tokyo.
>
> What support is given in the books for the statement, Tokyo is a crowded city?
>
> Do you think the books provide enough support for us to safely make such a statement? Why?

A variation of this procedure with younger students would be:

"Look through the two books that have been passed out to you. Which of the two books would be more helpful in helping us learn more about how people travel in downtown Tokyo? Why?"

137 Noting Main Ideas

Tape record a short reading selection. After listening to the recording, ask the students to list about five main ideas. After discussing and comparing individual efforts, ask several students to use their list of main ideas to retell the selection.

Follow-up

Consider having each student use his or her list of ideas and write the selection as presented.

After listening to a story, younger students could be led to fold a sheet of art paper into fourths and then draw four pictures that could be used to retell the story.

138 *Phrasing the Story*

Notetaking

Tape record a short selection from a social studies text. After the students have listened to the recording, distribute a list of about fifteen short phrases that are relevant to the selection. Have the students circle the best four or so phrases (or even create different ones) to be used in recalling the main points of the selection. Call on students to discuss their selections and their reasons for specific choices.

139 *Scrambled Phrases*

Sequencing

Assign a popular TV program for the students to view. Prepare a handout with a series of short phrases descriptive of the program, but out of sequence. Have the students cut out the phrases and rearrange them in the order of the program's presentation. Call on several students to refer to their outline and briefly to describe the program.

140 *Tag-Board Sequencing*

Sequencing

On tag-board strips prepare an outline for a short section of social studies content. Cut the outline into its separate sections and pin each section to a bulletin board area. After presenting the selection, involve the class in arranging the outline pieces into a workable sequence. Have several students use the outline to retell the story previously presented.

Note

A flannel board can be used instead of the bulletin board if you paste sections of sandpaper to the backs of the tag-board strips.

※ 141 *Organizing the Snapshots*

In some schools, equipment and funds are available for taking snapshots during the school year. If this is the case in your school, have students sequence the photo collection into bulletin board or scrapbook displays depicting the developing history of the school year.

Collecting Original Information

※ 142 *School Tour Data*

Tour the school with your students and have them look for any items of a particular shape (triangular, rectangular, etc.). This experience can prepare the students for other observational data collection activities such as touring the school to note specific examples of concepts like: groups, rules, interdependence, systems, division of labor.

Note

Consider assigning concepts for students to find examples of when going on a field trip.

※ 143 *Using Cassettes*

Hint

When collecting observational data, consider taking along a cassette tape recorder. For example, a student might record the following:

> "This is Leslie. I just observed an example of division of labor: One person took the person's money and another one prepared the food."

Separate tape cassettes can be used for each concept.

86   SECTION 1

✻ 144 *Sack Data*

This activity can help students learn to record their observations.

Place each item from a list like the following into separate sacks:

> A piece of candy
> 'Slime'
> A dead insect
> A small toy
> A quarter

Each sack is assigned a number and the top is folded over so that the contents cannot be seen. See Figure 144a. Volunteers are to select one sack apiece. Explain that the

Figure 144a

contents of the sack belongs to the one making the selection. All volunteers are then asked to leave the room until called back individually to make their selections. It is then explained to the remainder of the class that they are to observe the reaction of each person after discovering the contents of a particular selection. The observation is to be recorded by marking one of the three faces on the observation sheet (see Figure 144b).

Person observed	Observed reaction
Name _____	☺ ☹ ☹
Name _____	☺ ☹ ☹
Name _____	☺ ☹ ☹
Name _____	☺ ☹ ☹

Figure 144b

Note

Do not allow any of the students making selections to pick up the sack, touch the objects, or in any way indicate what is in the sack. Afterwards, list all of the items in the sacks on the board. Then have the students refer to their observational sheets and guess who selected which items, giving reasons for their answers.

145 *Self-Observation Data*

Students can be involved in collecting data on themselves through self-observation. The direction may be very simple: "List three different groups you were in today," or "List three rules you followed today at school."

☼ 146 *Animal Data*

Classroom animals can be used in the collection of observational data. For example, an ant farm might be observed for evidence of individuals within a group working together. A simple data form (see Figure 146, p. 89) might be used when studying the behavior of hamsters.

☼ 147 *Interview Data*

Consider the possibility of using the telephone to interview someone who is unable to visit the school. In some schools, speaker-phone systems have been installed that allow any person in a class to speak and be heard at the other end of the line without leaving the desk.

Hint

Be prepared for the interview. Involve the students in advance in deciding on the kinds of information they want and the necessary questions for getting such information.

☼ 148 *Primary Data*

Try to supplement a traditional assignment that has students going to textbooks and encyclopedias for information with an activity that involves the collection of primary data. For example, let us say that you are involved in a unit of study on communication. Parents and grandparents could serve as data sources for the following questions about radio:

> What were some of the radio programs you used to listen to when you were my age? Which of these were your favorites? Why?
>
> How was listening to radio when you were my age like looking at TV today? What are some differences?

(*continued* p. 90)

What time was it when you saw the hamster eat? _____

_____

What was the hamster eating? _____

What time was it when you saw the hamster exercising?

_____

What was the exercise? _____

What time was it when you saw the hamster sleeping?

_____

How long did you see the animal sleep? _____

Where did the hamster store food? _____

Where in the cage was the hamster sleeping? _____

_____

What did the hamster do when (something in the environment was changed)? _____

_____

Using your observations, write or tell one or two sentences about the behavior of hamsters. _____

_____

Figure 146

What are other things you remember about listening to radio? Do you miss those things? Why?

Note

When working with younger students, use of only the first question may be sufficient.

149 *Conceptual Data*

Using older people as data sources, consider how data generated from the following questions could lead to student statements around such concepts as change, norms, and role expectations:

What cars were popular when you were my age? What changes have been made in cars from those times to today?

What did you usually wear to school when you were my age?

What subjects do you remember studying in school when you were my age?

What were some of the things you used to do after school when you were my age?

What jobs did you have when you were my age?

150 *Rank-Order Data*

Students can collect data by administering rank-order questionnaires. However, keep the questionnaire as brief as possible; there is a tendency for teachers and students to collect so much data that the processing becomes unmanageable. The rank-order questionnaire can be as simple as the one in Figure 150.

151 *Attitudinal Data*

Besides rank-order questionnaires (Activity 150), additional procedures exist that students can readily employ in

Rank-order Questionnaire

Below are four activities. Select the one that is your favorite and write a *1* before it. Write a *2* before your second favorite, a *3* before your next choice, and finally a *4* before your last choice.

_____ Listening to records
_____ Watching TV
_____ Listening to the radio
_____ Reading a book you choose

Figure 150

collecting data concerning how individuals feel about various phenomena. A technique found repeatedly in the activities of this book is to have individuals indicate which of three faces in Figure 151 represent their feelings:

Such data can be collected in several ways. Questionnaires can be created and marked directly by the respondent or by someone using the questionnaire as an interview guide. Alternatively, responses can be tape recorded. This procedure allows all of the class members to get involved later in tallying the results.

152 "If They Were Here" Data

Involve students in thinking of questions they would pose to an individual *if* it were possible to interview that person.

Figure 151

Examples

> What are three questions you would ask Abraham Lincoln if he were here today? Why would you ask these particular questions?
>
> What questions would you ask an owner of the cargo that was thrown overboard at the Boston Tea Party?
>
> What questions would you want to ask the author of the selection we just read?

153 *Biographical Data*

Have students interview the person sitting next to them and then make a brief presentation to the rest of the class. The brief interview and presentation can revolve around such basic information as the other person's name, birthplace and date, number of family members, and interests. This is also a good ice breaker when group members are unfamiliar with one another.

Processing Information

154 *Human Graphs*

This is one suggestion for helping students begin to comprehend the rather abstract notion of graphing.

Ask each student to think of an answer to the following question:

> Where do you usually get your lunch on those days that you go to school:
> a. Bring your lunch from home?
> b. Go home for lunch?
> c. Buy your lunch at school?

Next, display a row of pictures that are representative of each of the response options for the question. Ask the students to line up (form a column) in front of the picture that goes with the response they have chosen. In essence, a human graph (histogram) will result. See Figure 154a. Ask individual students to back away from the lines of students and describe what they observe (make inferential statements).

Figure 154a

Now display a large sheet of butcher paper (perhaps 4′ × 6′). Using felt tip pens, clearly list the three response options. Have the separate lines of students approach the display, with each student taping a small square (2″ × 2″) of construction paper in the appropriate row. See Figure 154b, p. 94. Review with the students what each square of paper stands for and how the graph stands for the lines they were previously in. Have the class decide on a title for their graph as well as a key.

94 SECTION 1

>
> **Where We Get Our Lunch**
>
> □   □   □
>
> □   □   □
>
> □   □   □
>
> □
>
> Bring Lunch   Go Home   Buy

Figure 154b

155 *Row Holders*

This activity describes another procedure for working with graphs. Make a 'row holder' out of a strip of butcher paper approximately 6" × 36". Fold the strip of paper in half, lengthwise, and place several staples in both ends. Display individual row holders, one under the other, for each of the response options available for the question being posed, indicating a particular response option for each row. Have each student write his or her name on a 4" × 6" index card. After posing a question, such as the one used in the preceding activity, ask the students to deposit their cards in the appropriate row holder. See Figure 155, p. 95.

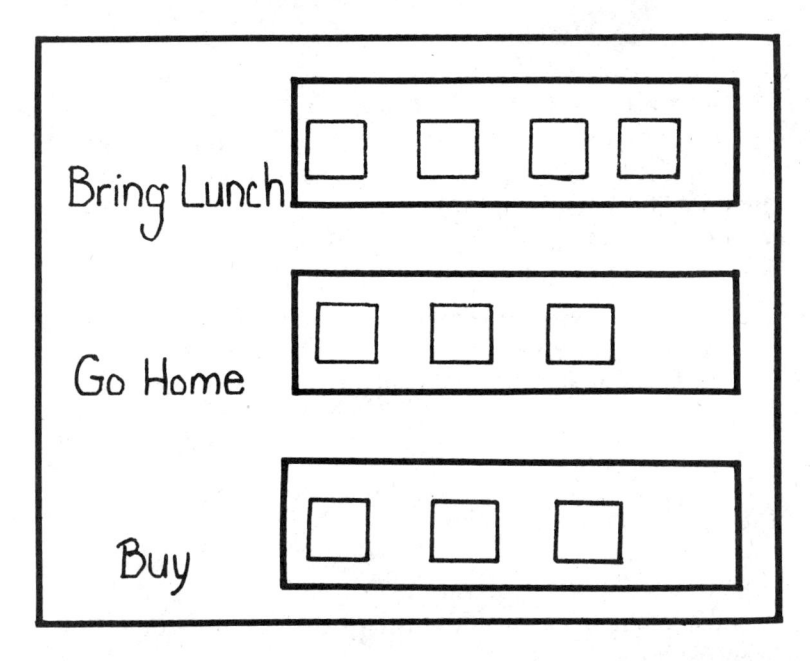

Figure 155

☼ **156 Student Recorders**

Questionnaire responses can sometimes be tape recorded rather than written. In processing such information, first display a large strip of butcher paper and list each of the response categories. Assign a student recorder to each response category. As the responses are played back from the recording, have the 'appropriate' recorder enter a tally mark on the chart.

☼ **157 Flow Charts**

Help students become familiar with flow charts and diagrams by having them list the steps involved in such simple activities as washing the dishes or cleaning the cage of a pet animal. Then ask them to draw a picture for each

96   SECTION 1

step, and when completed, to place the pictures in order. Consider having the students mount the pictures on a single sheet of paper and then number the proper picture sequence. The same procedures might then be applied to the typical events in the life of a student on a school day.

Older students can use descriptive phrases in place of drawing pictures and can become involved in creating flow charts to show such things as the sequence of events at the Battle of Lexington (even representing varied versions) or the sequence of activity involved in an automobile assembly line.

158   *Information Displays*

Sometimes lists of information in chart form are all that are needed to process and display information that has been gathered.

For example, let us suppose that the students have been involved in keeping track of the jobs they have done around the house over a period of several days. A chart like the one in Figure 158 would be an informative way to display the data.

159   *Picture Charts*

Young students might be asked to prepare a chart of the food they like by cutting pictures out of newspapers and magazines and pasting them to a sheet of paper. With teacher help, titles can be given to each chart.

160   *Human-Symbol Graphs*

Have all students form a line from tallest to shortest. Divide the line into thirds and measure the heights of the extremes for each third. Involve the class in creating a

Household Chores

Jobs	When I Did the Job
	Sun. Mon. Tues. Wed. Th. Fri. Sat.
Empty trash	
Wash dishes	
Set table	
Sweep	
Make my bed	
Babysit	
Take care of pets	
Water	

Figure 158

chart like the one shown in Figure 160, p. 98. As a follow-up activity, the procedure could be repeated with other classrooms and comparisons made between the data contained on the various charts.

Alternative

Rather than write out the range of heights for each third, cut out a butcher-paper outline for the persons at the height extremes. Display the appropriate outlines for each column of data.

161 *Student Data Processors*

Each week have the students select the best question that has been suggested for collecting data that can be graphed

98   SECTION 1

Heights of Students in Room 6

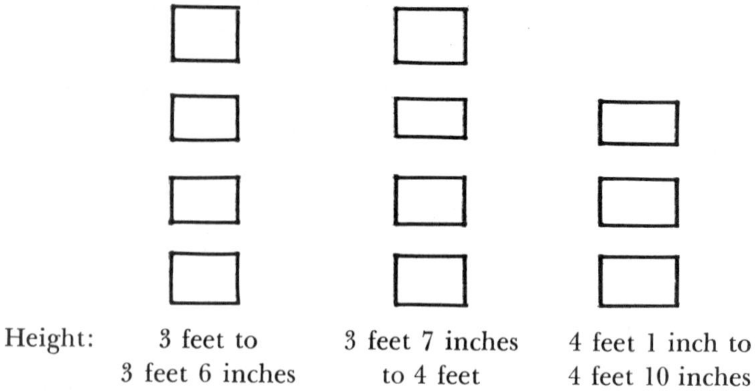

Height: 3 feet to   3 feet 7 inches   4 feet 1 inch to
          3 feet 6 inches   to 4 feet   4 feet 10 inches

Figure 160

(such as, Where do students go for lunch?). Place the student with the winning suggestion in charge of collecting and processing the data required, but offer personal help as well as classroom time for carrying out the needed procedures. Involve the rest of the class in these efforts.

Reporting

The following techniques are offered as alternatives, or supplements, to more traditional reporting procedures such as turning in a written report or having individuals read or present their findings to the rest of the class.

✺ 162   *Newscast*

A TV newsroom is used as the setting for presenting the report. One student serves as the anchor person and calls on various 'reporters on special assignment' to discuss specific segments of the findings. Props simulating microphones and TV cameras can help establish the environment for implementing this technique.

163 Press Conference

One person offers several preliminary remarks followed by questions from the press corps (the other members of the presenting group).

164 Skit

A short dramatization is written and presented that reflects the content of the report. The technique is especially good for comparing and contrasting the activities of various cultural groups as reflected in their families, schools, holidays and celebrations, belief systems, and forms of recreation.

165 Interest Centers

Charts, graphs, diagrams, maps, artifacts, and written selections pertinent to a particular topic or theme are displayed. Tape recorded segments and student 'guides' are used to involve the visitors with the content of the center.

166 Courtroom

This procedure is especially effective for the presentation of controversial issues.

For example, 'lawyers' might argue before a 'judge' on whether the people involved in the Boston Tea Party should be punished. 'Eye witnesses' and 'expert witnesses' could be interwoven into the courtroom drama.

167 Circle Tap In

This procedure is especially good for discussing and developing issues.

Two circles of students are formed, one circle within

the other. In the smaller, inner circle, about three to four students take turns offering opinions on an issue. Only members of the inner circle are allowed to speak, but members of the larger outer circle may get involved by tapping on the shoulder of an inner circle member. The person who is tapped then moves to the outer circle. It is sometimes suggested that some members of the inner circle be designated as immune from being tapped (such as those students who are mainly responsible for the presentation).

168 *TV Quiz Game*

A master of ceremonies poses questions to contestants about a particular topic. Winners compete with 'new' contestants.

169 *Commercial Time-Outs*

Advertising posters and presentations are used to:

> Present various sides of a controversy
> Sell specific products of a country
> Publicize an up-coming holiday in another country

This presentation technique can easily be integrated with other techniques already described (such as *Newscast,* Activity 162; *Press Conference,* Activity 163; and *TV Quiz Game,* Activity 168).

170 *Audio-Visual Media*

Encourage students to use a variety of audio-visual media in their presentations. With assistance, students might make overlays for use on overhead projectors; tape record background music or on-the-spot interviews; and speak from charts, graphs, and maps. Demonstrate and list the audio-visual possibilities before the report is finalized.

171 *Special Edition*

Besides the variety of presentation techniques available, students should also be advised on additional alternative forms the report might take.

Examples

- A special edition of a newspaper containing relevant articles, editorials, etc.
- A photo essay consisting of snapshots, newspaper and magazine photographs, as well as drawings
- Shoebox collages, in which pictures are pasted to the outside surfaces of the shoe boxes
- Models
- Dioramas
- Roller movies
- Diaries
- Slide presentations

MAPS, GLOBES, SPACE UTILIZATION

RATIONALE

Historically, map and globe skills have enjoyed a prominent role in the social studies. Textbooks abound with map and globe activities and supportive films and other media are also readily available. No attempt has been made in this section to replace the instructional ideas and materials that already exist. However, what should be noted, as reflected in several of the suggested activities, is how a study of maps and globes can be expanded to involve students in a consideration of how persons use their space—a pervasive theme of geographical inquiry. Furthermore, as reflected in Activity 146, in which students observe the behavior of animals, it can be noted that meaningful observations and study can also be made of non-human, as well as of human uses of environmental space.

Activities

172 *Population Patterns*

Referring to maps and globes, have the students locate the nearest line of latitude to their city. They then can locate the countries and major population centers around the world that are located at the same latitude.

Focus questions

How are the places located on the same latitude alike in terms of climate? population? products?

How are they different?

173 *The Big Ten*

Using the *World Almanac* and maps and globes, have the students locate the ten largest cities in the world.

SKILLS   103

The following questions can be used for class discussion or to provide the basis for a worksheet:

1. How many of the cities are found in the Western hemisphere? The Eastern hemisphere?
2. How many cities are located north of the equator? South of the equator?
3. *Optional:* Categorize the cities in terms of the following criteria:
   a. Western hemisphere, north of the equator
   b. Western hemisphere, south of the equator
   c. Eastern hemisphere, north of the equator
   d. Eastern hemisphere, south of the equator
4. What are possible explanations for your findings (i.e., as found in questions 1–3)?

174   The Shortest Trip

Using a globe and a length of string, have students locate the shortest route and the mileage between such locations as:

Los Angeles to Tokyo
New York to Hong Kong
Chicago to Rio de Janeiro

Optional

Change mileage to metric equivalents.
See Figure 174, p. 104.

175   Traveling From Large to Small

Involve groups of students in planning a trip between places such as those listed below. The trips are to take the least amount of time possible. Also note that for each pair of cities listed, one is a large population center and the

Figure 174

other is quite small. Thus, various kinds of maps and atlases will be needed since several of the cities will not appear on some maps. Also, try to line up airline flight schedules that can be used in the trip planning, as well as brochures from various car rental agencies. Train and bus schedules could also be made available.

List of Trips

1. New York — Winnemucca, Nevada
2. Los Angeles — Witt, Illinois
3. Chicago — Fallbrook, California
4. St. Louis — Hibbing, Minnesota
5. Minneapolis — Americus, Georgia
6. Washington, D.C. — Palm Springs, California
7. Seattle, Washington — Bumble Bee, Arizona

8. San Francisco   Aspen, Colorado
9. Detroit   Black Rock, Arkansas

Guide questions

What are the total number of miles (air as well as land) for the trip between 'your' two cities? Estimate the least amount of time 'your' trip will take. (Note: Encourage the students to study the schedules for direct flights and to estimate driving times as well as flight times.)

Optional

What will be the transportation costs (one way) for your trip?

Extend this activity by focusing on such questions as:

What differences, if any, are there in the ease of traveling east to west or west to east rather than north to south or south to north in the United States?
What is the evidence for your response?
What is the evidence that some small towns are easier to get to than others?

(Help the students see relationships between small town accessibility and such factors as proximity to a large population center, or being a tourist attraction such as Palm Springs or Aspen.)

176 *Main Street*

On a sheet of butcher paper, draw a large map that shows the main streets of your school's neighborhood. Mark the school's location. Distribute a dittoed outline of a house and have each student write his or her name and address. After cutting out the outline, students can pin it in the correct location on the butcher paper map. See Fig. 176, p. 106.

106   SECTION 1

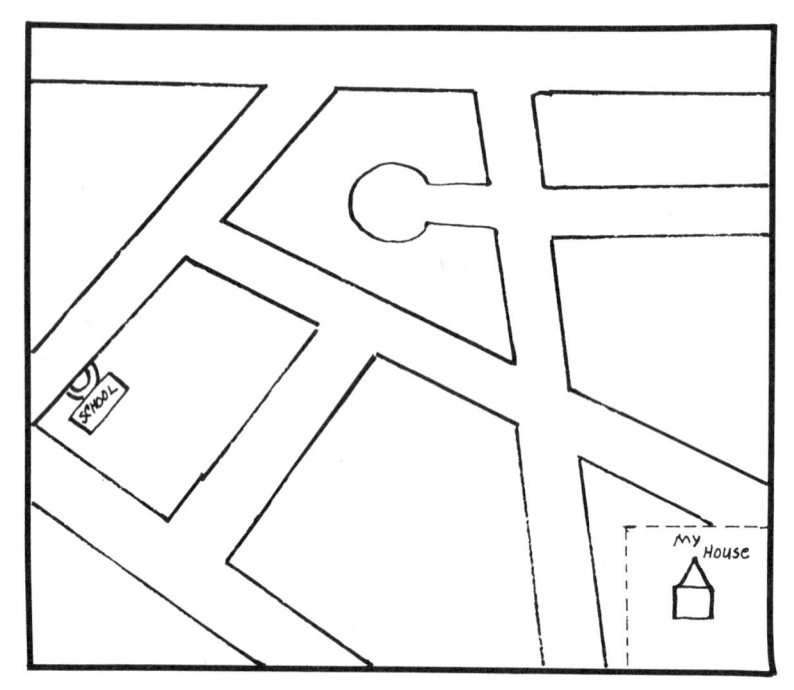

Figure 176

Follow-up procedures

>Have each student use the map and decide the best route for going from home to school.
>
>Ask students to locate the homes that are closest and farthest from school.
>
>Locate all homes on the same side of the street as school; across the street, etc.

Alternative procedure

If practical, have the students bring in photographs of their homes and pin these to the wall map of the neighborhood.

177   Creating Map Symbols

Using a wall map like the one described in Activity 176, have the class create and locate symbols for various neigh-

Figure 177

borhood phenomena. Include a key on the map for the symbols. See Figure 177, above.

Such phenomena as the following might be located:

    A park   Student road crossings
    Churches   Bus stops
    Supermarkets   Bus loading area
    Fire hydrants   Trees
    Crosswalks   Public benches, etc.

178 *Map Hunt Game*

Play the *Map Hunt Game*.

On butcher paper or tag-board, draw an outline map of the classroom, including the location of desks, tables, doors, closets, animal cages, book shelves, etc. See Figure

108 SECTION 1

178. A volunteer leaves the room. One of the remaining students is chosen to hide an object (such as a chalk eraser) somewhere in the classroom and then pin a small card on the map representative of where the object was hidden. The volunteer re-enters to read the map and locate the object. Add map detail as students gain in their sophistication to read and interpret the map.

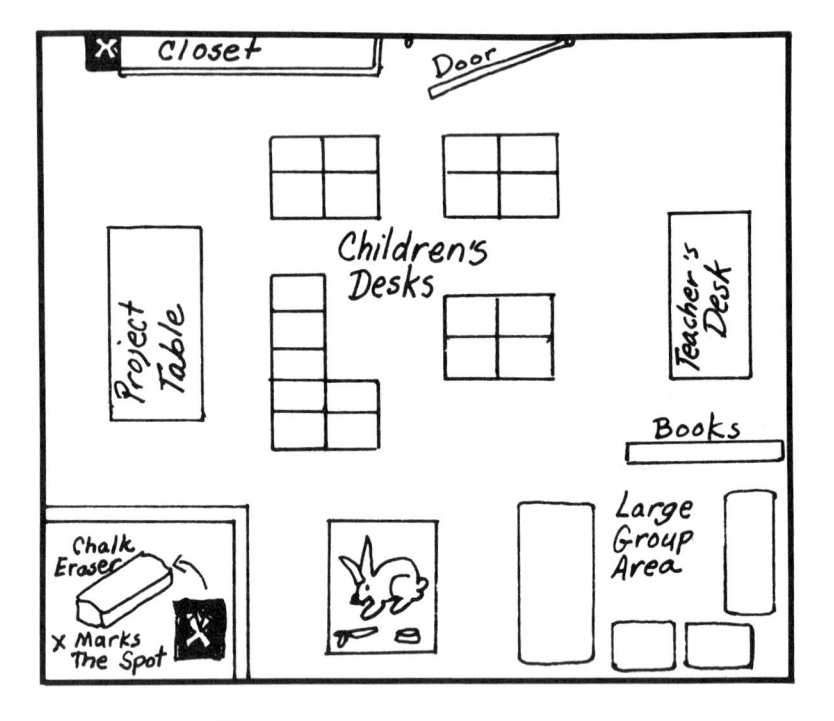

Figure 178

Alternative

Choose several teams. Have one team hide the object and locate it on the map. A representative of the other team has two minutes to locate the object. Finding the object within the time allowance results in a point being awarded to that person's team. A further modification is to award points according to how long it takes to locate the object: less than 30 seconds—5 points; 31 seconds to 1 minute—

3 points; more than 1 minute and up to 2 minutes—1 point.

☼ 179 *Use of Environments*

Have students draw simple maps to show how the space within specific environments is used.

For example, a map might be drawn to show where the hamster:

a. Sleeps
b. Stores food
c. Exercises
d. Drinks
e. Eats
f. Takes care of bodily functions

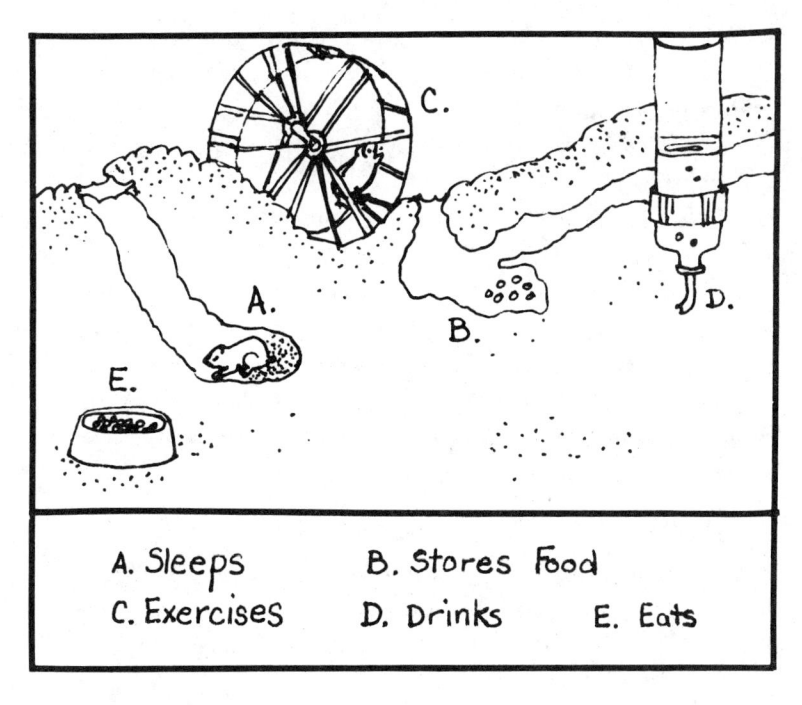

Figure 179

Follow-up possibility

Repeat the procedure on several occasions to determine if there are variations in the space uses for a specific environment over a period of time.

Note

Help younger students decide on what symbols will be used to represent various phenomena. Dittoed copies of what is decided on could be distributed when it comes time to draw the map.

You may prefer to involve the class in drawing one large map on the chalk board.

180 *Space Use Proposals*

Allow groups of students to explore the school and make specific recommendations regarding the best location for such items as:

   A new kindergarten room
   A new set of swings for the playground
   A new bicycle rack
   A place for teacher volunteers to listen to children read.

The groups can report back and present the various alternatives they considered and the specific reasons for their particular selection from among the alternatives.

Modification

Have several groups offer their proposals before a student 'space-use commission.' The commission can report to the rest of the class on what arguments for space use they found particularly appealing.

181 *Shopping Center Plan*

Present the following situation:

A new shopping center is being planned and is to be located at (try to name a specific location in your community with which the children are familiar). The entire center is to have no more than five stores.

Now involve the class in deciding which five stores (either specific names or types of stores are satisfactory) should be in the shopping center. Reasons should be given with each suggestion.

Follow-up

Provide a variety of boxes and have groups of students set up the arrangement for the five stores previously decided on. Have the groups present their plans to the class. See Figure 181.

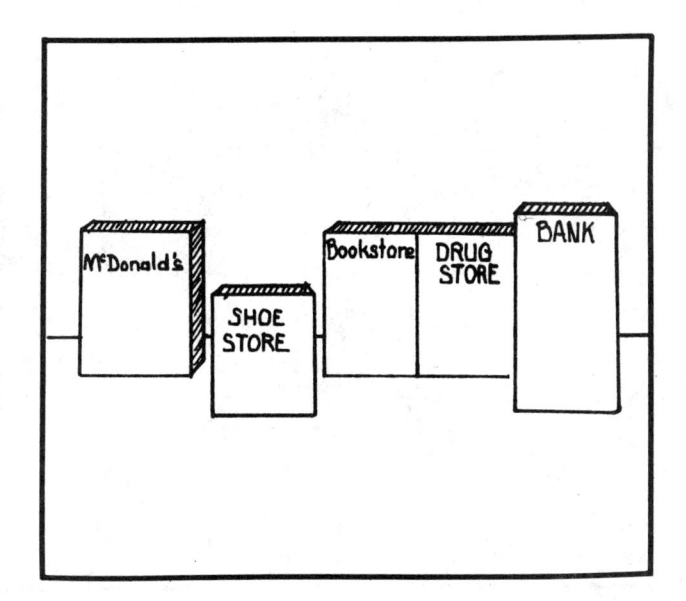

Figure 181

☼ 182 *Team Location*

Have groups of students make presentations on where and why the next major league baseball, football, basketball, or soccer team should be located.

☼ 183 *Classroom Demography*

Generate a list of all the cities in which the students have lived. On a large outline map of the United States, locate each city and place a pin for each person who has lived in the location. See Figure 183.

Follow-up questions

> What are the most popular cities in which students in our class have lived? Why might this be so?

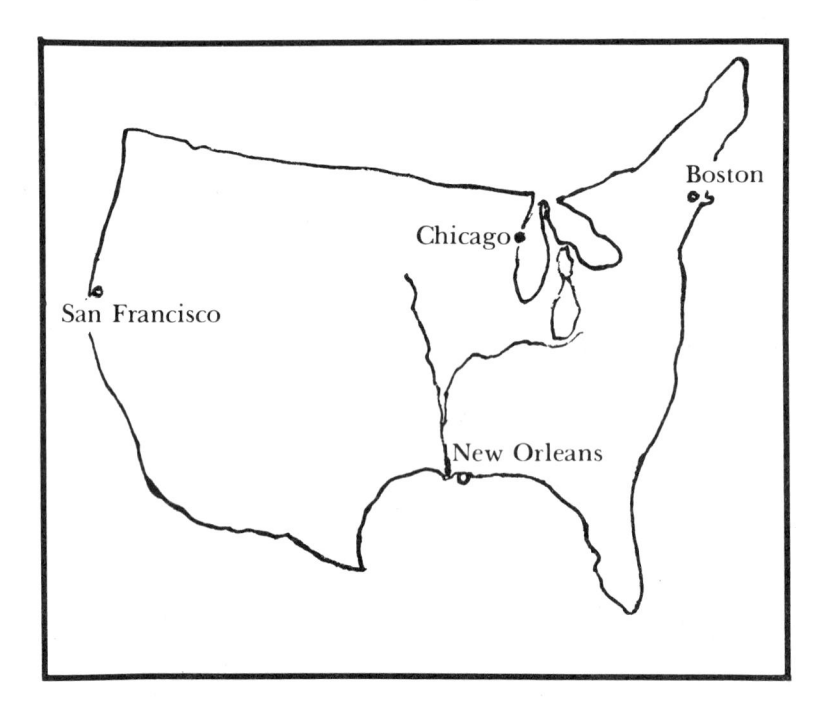

Figure 183

What states, other than the one we live in now, have been the most 'popular'? Guess at why this might be so.

184 *Site Selection*

Involve students in making suggestions on where in the school neighborhood would be the best location for a particular structure or utilization, such as a new fast-food outlet, a new laundromat, a new park.

When a particular site selection involves the removal of an existing structure, the students should be able to argue that the negative effects of such a change are more than offset by the new structure.

Similarly, students should offer specific reasons for their choices (for example, many people pass that intersection; the noise is far enough away from the nearest homes; etc.).

Students could dramatize the roles of real estate brokers and business owners in weighing and deciding among alternative possibilities.

185 *Neighborhood Ads*

Have students reflect on why people might live where they do, by creating ads for their own neighborhood. See Figure 185, p. 114. Display the ads and involve the class in making a list of the reasons reflected. Also ask for additional reasons that were not depicted.

186 *Shoe-Box Models*

Let students create models representing such structures as: the school, the classroom, their bedroom. Shoe boxes provide a good starting point for such model-building activity. See Figure 186, p. 114.

114   SECTION 1

Figure 185

Figure 186

TIME AND CHRONOLOGY

RATIONALE

It is extremely difficult for many young learners to understand a chronological sequence, especially when the events occurred out of their lifetimes. Dealing with such abstractions might be helped if events within the students' own lifetime were first instructionally emphasized and then used as a reference point for interpreting dates or periods outside of their life experiences. For example, students might first sequence events in their own day, during the week, and during and throughout the school year. Later, the students could study how their parents spent their time at comparable ages. Parents could even be used as a standard of time and events described in terms of having taken place one, two, or three 'parents' ago.

Characteristic of the activities in this section is an involvement of the students with chronological and time skills that draw on data from the present, on the premise that such experiences can prove helpful when sorting through phenomena that is past or future oriented.

Activities

✿ 187 *Time Line*

Have the students cut out pictures of human activity, using magazines, newspapers, and catalogs. The students can then arrange the pictures on a time line drawn on butcher paper and displayed on the wall. Divide the time line according to such time reference periods as: Before starting school, Going to School, Married—own family, and Grandparents. See Figure 187.

Such categories provide a personal reference point for the students, as opposed to the more abstract use of number of years (five years ago, five years from now, etc.). Frequently a picture will include individuals of more than

116   SECTION 1

| Before School | Going to School | Married—Own Family | Grandparents |

Figure 187

one age group. In such instances, have the students draw a circle around the individual they want to highlight for purposes of placement on the time line.

After completion of the time line, involve the students in describing the activities that are shown and in making comparisons between the categories.

188   *Time Line and Me*

In dealing with past events, try to help the students establish a personal frame of reference. For example, events, topics, or phenomena might be placed within the categories shown in Figure 188.

As the students begin to relate to such categories, you might wish to state that category (B) might mean about thirty years ago and (C) about thirty more years past that, for a total of sixty years from the present. You could also list the approximate dates for the (B) and (C) categories. However, neither the listing of the number of years or the specific dates is crucial; allow the students to deal intuitively with the categories.

Notice how a time line and its categories as suggested here might be used to organize various items (pictures, writing selections, artifacts, models, replicas) around such

| Right now: I am ____ years old (A) | When my parents were my age (B) | When my grandparents were my age (C) |

Figure 188

topics as: toys, entertainment, wars, inventions, clothing, communication, transportation, recreation, school, jobs, roles, music, art.

189 *Time Mobiles*

Alternatives to drawing time lines include:

- Constructing mobiles for each of several time periods
- Using the sides of a shoe box for specific time periods and creating collages with appropriate pictures and drawings
- Creating display tables showing various period groupings

190 *Changes Depicted*

Start picture files of the changes that have taken place over the years within such topics as those generated in a preceding activity (such as toys, entertainment, wars, etc.). Have a student randomly draw from three to five pictures from a particular file and arrange them in a sequence on the chalk tray (see Figure 190, p. 118). Ask the student to state the reasons for the picture sequence, or call on another student to offer possible explanations.

Note

Students can be involved in locating and cutting out pictures around specific topics that you might use in creating picture files.

191 *Collecting Change Data*

Start a class scrapbook at the beginning of the school year. Each week, ask the class to decide on one main event that best represents that school week and to think of and create

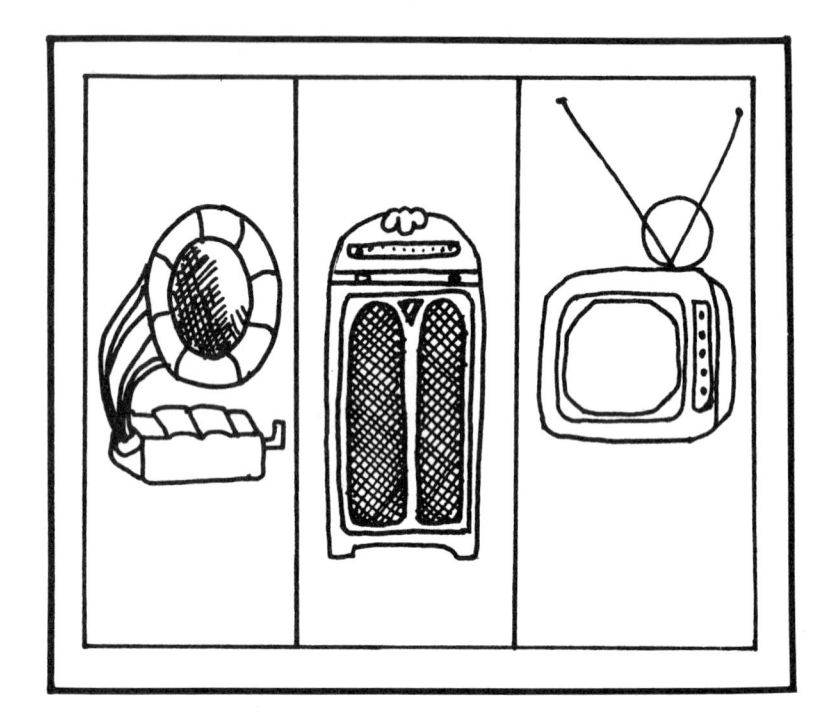

Figure 190

an entry (such as a drawing, picture, or several descriptive sentences) to capture the event. Each week, ask a student to refer to all of the entries and to re-create what has happened in the classroom during the current school year.

192 Short Time Lines

Younger students should be introduced to time lines that reflect short periods of times and personal experiences. On a sheet of butcher paper about 4 feet in length draw a time line for one week's duration. See Figure 192.

At the end of each day, involve the class in thinking of one or two key events of the day that might be entered

Monday	Tuesday	Wednesday	Thursday	Friday

Figure 192

in the appropriate space on the time line. At the end of the week, call on various individuals to use the time line to tell what happened in the classroom during the week.

193 When Is "I Love Lucy"?

Make available to the class TV program listings for your area. Consider allowing the students to work in groups of two or three. Have each group select a favorite program and respond to questions like the following (let us assume that the children live in an eastern time zone):

When you look at the program you selected, what time will it be in San Francisco? in Miami? in St. Louis? in Denver?

Assuming that the program you selected comes on at the same time period as in our city, what time will it be *here* when the same program is being shown in Los Angeles? in Seattle? in Houston? in Oklahoma City? in Cincinnati?

Alternative

Set up and label four clock faces as shown in Fig. 193, p. 120.

Allow students to indicate their responses to the questions by manipulating the clock hands.

194 TV Time

Activity 193 can be turned into the game *TV Time* requiring the use of several skills.

120 SECTION 1

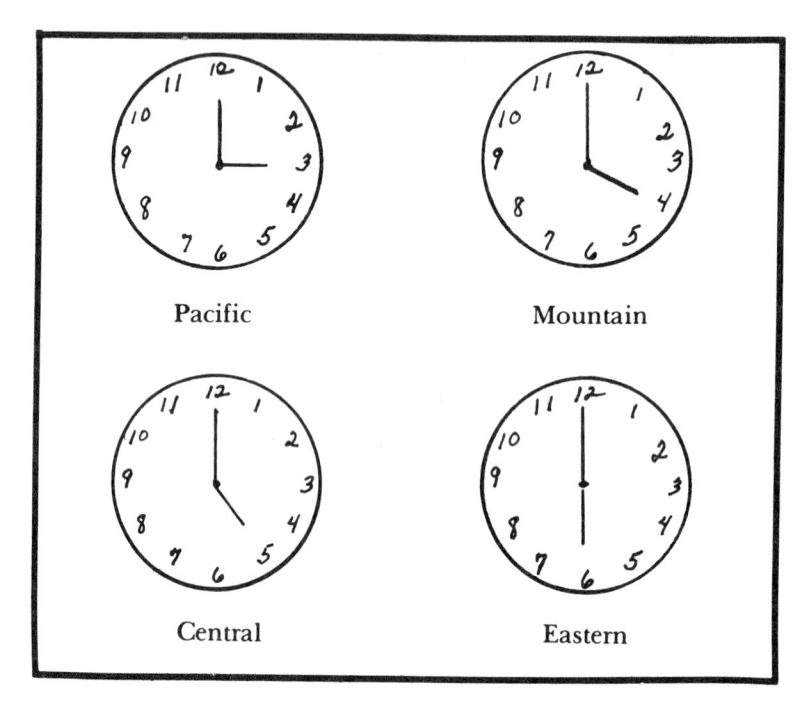

Figure 193

A particular program is announced. A team member then looks up the program, indicating the time, day of week, and channel for the program *and* the page of the TV listings on which such information is found. Then the same student, or another team member, manipulates the various clock faces to indicate what time it will be in different time zones when the program is shown locally. Points can be awarded for each correct response.

LISTENING

RATIONALE

Although we as teachers may admonish students "to listen" or "to pay attention," we frequently overlook the possibility that listening is a skill that can be improved through direct instructional intervention. Similarly, we might even be teaching certain students *not* to listen through such subtle cues as infrequently requiring them to respond to a question or seldom asking them to comment on what someone other than the teacher has presented.

Activities

195 *Communication Chains*

Tape record a short statement ("Charles lost his lunch money on the way to school yesterday") and whisper it to a student. Have that student pass the statement along to the nearest student who, in turn, whispers it to the next nearest student, etc. Ask the last student to repeat aloud what was heard. Then play the tape recording and have the class compare it to what the last person heard, offering possible reasons for any differences. Also, try to trace at which points in the communication chain the statement got changed.

196 *Sound Identification*

Ask the students to close their eyes and attempt to identify specific sounds you will make. After two or three sounds are made (refer to list for several possibilities) call on students to make identifications as well as to discuss why they think their guesses are accurate.

List of Sounds
1. Book hitting the floor.
2. Opening, closing a door.
3. Breaking the point of a pencil.
4. Moving a desk.
5. Running the faucet or drinking fountain.
6. Clapping eraser against the chalk board.
7. Sharpening a pencil.

197 *School Sounds*

Have students generate lists of school sounds (such as playground noise, ringing bells, picking up books, voice on the intercom, etc.); home sounds, church sounds, etc.

198 *Student-to-Student Listening*

After a class presentation (a student report, someone's statement of a position during a class discussion, the showing of a film, the completion of a reading selection), involve individual students in summarizing and reacting to what they have heard. For example, let us say that students are taking turns summarizing their reports. On the board, you have written the following questions:

1. What are the main ideas of the report you just heard? What new information did you get from the report?
2. How is the report you just heard like that of [name of someone else who has already reported]? How is the report different?
3. What are two things you especially like about the report?
4. With which parts of the report do you agree or disagree? Why?

Students are then called on to select one or two of the questions, read them, and respond.

Note

These questions reflect a 'reporting' environment. However, the procedure is equally applicable to a variety of instructional situations (such as viewing a film or filmstrip; listening to a guest speaker, a recording, a class discussion, etc.)

Section 2

CONCEPTS

RATIONALE

Concepts can be thought of as the names we give to things, objects, and ideas that share common characteristics. The book you are now reading is one example of the concept, *book*, because it has such characteristics as pages, binding, and a cover, which are germane to the concept. We can also think of concepts as categories. Indeed, we categorize our ideas, objects, and the phenomena about us on the basis of a commonality of attributes.

Concepts are intellectual abstractions. We cannot physically hold the concept, *book*—we must hold and apply its conceptual attributes through our intellect. Thus, the book you are now reading is not the concept of book, but rather, an instance of the concept.

Several other characteristics of concepts should also be understood. For example, concepts are creations of human beings. As human beings, we are continuously creating new categories or concepts, or reshaping existing ones, in order accurately to reflect expansions or changes in knowledge. Astronaut, skateboard, space shuttle, solid-state, and chips (computer-type), are representative of recent conceptual creations—or at least significant modifications of previous uses.

Concepts are learned, not acquired automatically as a result of being born human. You know that the book you are now reading is an example of the concept book, because earlier you learned the salient characteristics of *bookism*.

Concepts exist on various levels of complexity and inclusiveness. *Book* is a rather low level, simple concept (although it might not have appeared that way to you when you were much younger and were sifting through and learning the essential attributes of the concept). Higher order concepts from the social sciences include those used as topics in this section: rules, conflict, goods/services, learning, communication, and technology. Such concepts serve as major foci for the understandings within various social science disciplines and in that sense might be thought of as *key* concepts. Proponents of a conceptual approach in social studies education would maintain that to acquire understandings of the key concepts within the social science disciplines (anthropology, economics, etc.) is to know the essence of those disciplines.

Through an instructional emphasis on conceptual understandings, the teacher can help the learner acquire *relationships* among otherwise disparate pieces of information. Knowledge is pieced together as it relates to specific concepts, rather than left fragmented and isolated from any unifying theme. Thus, students might role play various *conflict* situations, not merely to discuss immediate solutions, but also better to relate to the *conflicts* involved in the Boston Tea Party, or between present-day environmentalists and developers.

Instructional activities are suggested for a few of the key concepts within several of the social science disciplines. However, the key concepts that are treated are among those most frequently identified and used in social studies instructional materials and programs currently available.

Rules

☼ **199 School Rules**

Involve the students in generating a list of all school rules for each of the following locations: classroom, halls, bathrooms, playground.

Follow-up questions

How are such rules learned? Who probably made up the rules?

Why have these rules?

What would it be like in each of these locations if there were no rules? How do you know?

How do new rules get started?

☼ **200 Rule Observations**

Drawing from a list of rules (like those generated in Activity 199), have a small group of students (two or three) go to specific school locations (hallway, playground, cafeteria) and record their observations of instances where rules are not being followed (see Figure 200a, p. 128). Confine the observations around a few specific rules and consider using an observation form like the one shown in Figure 200b.

Ask the observers to report their data (how many tallies did they mark for Rule 1 on the sheet?) and then describe the observations (such as, the rule that was broken most often was "Don't crowd in line"). Then consider the following questions:

128   SECTION 2

Figure 200a

Observation form for the cafeteria

Date _____ AM or PM

Mark an X in the box when you see someone not following the rules

Rule
1. Don't crowd in line. →
2. Don't throw food. →
3. Don't push in line. →
4. Return empty tray to → checkout counter. →

Figure 200b

Which rule was broken the most?
What might be reasons for this rule's being broken most often?
Is it still a good rule or should it maybe be done away with? Why?
If it is a good rule, then what might be done so that fewer students break it?
What should we do to see that our suggestions are tried out?

Note

If a class suggestion is implemented, then an observation team might return at a later date to the cafeteria and again record behavior. The results can give some general indication of whether their implemented suggestions have had an effect.

201 *Create A Rule*

Ask the students to imagine that they could have one new rule set up for the classroom.

What would the rule be? Why?
Which of the rules suggested are the best ones? Why?
What would be the benefits of the new rules?
What would have to be given up if the new rules were used?
What would it take to get the new rules 'passed'?
How would any new rule be enforced?
How would it be decided whether the new rules were 'good' rules?

202 *Observing Personal Rules*

Pass out a dittoed sheet requesting student data on such daily routines as when dinner is ordinarily eaten or the

130 SECTION 2

usual bedtime.[1] The students can be involved in graphing the data (see processing information section of this book) and in drawing inferences from the processed data (see section on making inferences).

Then use such questions as:

> What 'rules' are 'behind' these results? (e.g., "We eat dinner at 6:00 PM," "We eat dinner when my dad gets home," "I must be in bed with the lights off by 8:30.")
> Who made up these rules that you follow?
> What happens when you do not follow them?
> Do you think they are good rules? Why?
> When will you have more to say regarding the rules for your behavior?
> Why will this happen?

203 *Rules of the Road*

Secure multiple copies of your state's driver's test manual and have the students find specific rules covering such items as: making a left- or right-hand turn; parking time limits; speed limits on highways, in school zones, or in residential areas; approaching a crosswalk. Similarly, published rules could be used for driving a moped or bicycle.

Follow-up questions

> Is it really necessary to have such rules? Why?
> Why couldn't we just let people do what they felt was all right and not have lists of rules?

204 *Rule Enforcement*

Invite a law officer into the classroom to explain the local rules for such activity as riding a bicycle or walking along

---

1. Ryan, Frank L., and Arthur K. Ellis *Instructional Implications of Inquiry.* Englewood Cliffs, N.J.: Prentice-Hall Inc., 1974. Pp. 7, 8.

and crossing streets. Ask the officer to give reasons why he or she thinks such rules are needed and to describe what has happened when people chose *not* to follow the rules.

205 'Hard' Rules

Ask the principal, yard teacher, road guard, or bus driver to visit the classroom and discuss the rules they think are especially important as they try to do their jobs.

> Which of the rules are the hardest to enforce? Why?
> What are some of the worries they have when certain rules are not followed?

206 No-Rules Hour

Draw from the students a list of classroom rules ordinarily followed. Then have a no-rules hour during which students *and* the teacher can talk when they feel like it, wander around the room at will, read a book during math instruction—that is, generally disregard the previously listed classroom rules.

Follow-up questions

> Which of the listed classroom rules did you not follow?
> What did you gain by not following these rules? What did you lose?
> What was the classroom like without the rules?
> Which rules did you follow even though you didn't have to? Why?

Conflict

207 News Conflicts

Ask students to bring in newspaper articles, cartoons, and photographs that indicate a conflict (see Fig. 207, p. 132).

132 SECTION 2

Figure 207

Have each reporter state what the conflict is and how it might be, or already has been, resolved (perhaps by someone else, such as a judge, referee, umpire, or king). Some groups of students could also indicate if the means of taking care of the conflict were violent or nonviolent and offer suggestions for taking care of the conflict.

208 *Alternative History*

Have students write a paragraph describing alternative ways for working out such historical conflicts as the Battle of Lexington, the taking of land from the Indians by the colonists, and British taxation without representation. Presentation of alternative histories might include short skits, rewritten newspaper accounts, debates between the principles involved, mock courtroom scenes, political cartoons, and/or exchanges of letters.

209 *Personal Conflict*

Involve the students in brainstorming the conflicts/disagreements they have had with: brothers and sisters; parents; classmates; teachers. Discuss various ways to handle such conflicts (who to go to, when they might handle it on their own, etc.).

210 *TV Disagreements*

Assign the class the task of viewing a segment of a TV program such as *The Waltons* in order to identify a main conflict around which the story develops.
    Also ask:

How was the conflict taken care of?
What are other ways the conflict could have been handled?
In your opinion, are your suggestions for taking care of the conflict better than the ones shown in the program? Why?

211 *Conflict Role Playing*

Introduce short case studies that involve conflicts and have students role play toward a solution. Seven examples of case studies that might be appropriate for this activity are listed here.

1. Cars driven by Mrs. Smith and Mrs. Jones have collided. Each driver claims that the other person is at fault.
2. Mr. Mason thinks that Mr. Sumner's backyard fence

134   SECTION 2

is too high; and besides, it blocks his view of the ocean.
3. Mrs. Sheldon feels that the grocery store clerk has not given her the correct change.
4. The yard teacher tells Lance's classroom teacher that he was fighting on the playground. Lance was really trying to break up a fight between Matt and Sam.
5. Darren is waiting in line to play four-square when his teacher asks him to do an errand. When he returns he goes to the front of the line, claiming that he would have been there by now if he hadn't been asked to do the errand. Others in line say that he should go to the end of the line.
6. Mr. and Mrs. Howe want to build an apartment house on several acres of orange groves they own. Their neighbors object.
7. Jim and Mary O'Brien disagree on whose turn it is to take out the trash.

After each case study is enacted, ask:

How was the conflict taken care of? (by those involved? by "others"? fighting? peacefully?)
What are other ways it might have been handled?
How would you have solved the problem? Why?
Why is it that we sometimes allow others (parents, teachers) to decide how to take care of a conflict?

Consider having additional volunteers role play the same case studies, but using a different resolution of the conflict.

Goods/Services

☼ 212 *Yellow Pages*

Have groups of students use the telephone Yellow Pages and list the kinds of services included.

Suggestion

Assign specific sections of the Yellow Pages to each group such as pages 20–30, or the letter *R:* refuse removal, registered nurses, rehabilitation services, rental collection service. Compare the services available in a small community with those in larger communities as reflected in the listings in different sets of Yellow Pages.

213 *"Extra" Services in the Air*

Select a situation in which the price of a service is the same for competing companies (such as the cost of a flight from Los Angeles to New York). Collect advertising for the competing companies and list and compare the 'extra' services claimed by each company (in-flight movies, special meals, attractive flight attendants, easy check-in service, on-time flights, friendliness of employees, wide seating, special lounges, stereo music, experienced pilots, convenient schedules).
  Ask:

  Why do the competing companies make these 'extra' claims about their service?
  Which of the claims could you actually check out if you were to take a particular company's flight?
  Which claims could not be checked out merely by taking the flight (pilot experience, on-time record for a series of flights, expertise and experience of the mechanics).

214 *Other 'Extras'*

Alternative to Activity 213: Compare the 'extra' services offered by banks or by savings and loan institutions.

215 *Goods vs. Services*

Cut out the advertising (excluding the classified ads) of the daily paper. Hang two sheets of butcher paper (approximately 3 feet in length) on a wall, labeling one sheet 'Goods' and the other 'Services.' After a student determines whether a particular ad is oriented more toward goods or services, have someone paste or tape it to the appropriate sheet of butcher paper. Such a procedure allows the students to make statements regarding the relative space devoted to ads for goods or services on a particular day. The butcher sheets can be dated and the results compared with other days of the week and other times of the year.

216 *Servicing the Goods*

Have students gather ads oriented toward goods and determine if promises of services are also mentioned (new car dealer promises excellent maintenance and repair service, clothing store offers free alterations, TV store includes a 90-day service warranty with the purchase of each new TV, plumbing shop that sells as well as services). See Fig. 216, p. 137.

217 *Shopping-Center Tour*

Tour the stores and businesses within a nearby shopping complex, determining whether a particular establishment deals primarily in goods or services (or both) and the kinds of jobs required. An observation form (see Figure 217, p. 138) should facilitate the implementation of this activity.

Older students can maintain individual observation sheets, or work in groups of two or three to collect data. With younger children, the teacher can serve as the recorder. After the observation trip, discuss the various establishments in terms of being oriented toward goods and services and the number and kinds of jobs involved.

CONCEPTS 137

Figure 216. (Reprinted by permission of Olken's, Inc., Wellesley, Mass.)

Shopping Observation Form

Business/Store	Goods	Services	Jobs
J's Variety	✓		Clerks, managers, stockperson
Farley's Pharmacy	✓		(Same as for J's) pharmacist
Fancy Poodle Care		✓	
Big John's Hamburgers	✓		
A & J Tax Preparation		✓	
Bright's Dry Cleaning		✓	

Figure 217

218 *Sales Presentations*

Drawing from the same types of businesses (banks, groceries, new cars), assign specific companies to individual students for making sales presentations on why their company should be chosen over a competitor's. Ask the consumers (the other students) to indicate which part of each presentation they found particularly appealing. Did the presenter emphasize the quality of goods or services?

219 *Government Services*

Have the students identify services that are provided by the local government. See Figure 219, p. 139.
   Possibilities include:

        Fire protection
        Police protection

CONCEPTS 139

Figure 219

Trash pick-up
Public transportation

Ask: Do you think it would be better to have several different fire companies in our neighborhood, just as we have different kinds of gas stations? Why?

Try to have the students think of positive as well as negative consequences.

Learning

220 *Prior Learnings*

Have each student bring in several pictures showing activities that he or she has learned. The pictures might in-

140   SECTION 2

clude actual snapshots of learning how to walk or ride a bike, but also could include any picture showing activity they have mastered. Ask individuals to share their pictures and indicate the activity they have learned as well as who helped them learn. Consider providing bulletin board space for individual displays.

☼ 221 *Recalling/Predicting Learnings*

Divide a bulletin board space into three sections labelled: Learnings We Already Have; Learnings We Will Have Before Leaving [Elementary School, High School]; Those Who Have Helped Us Learn. See Figure 221. Students can bring in magazine and newspaper photographs, snapshots, or their own drawings, and place them in the appropriate

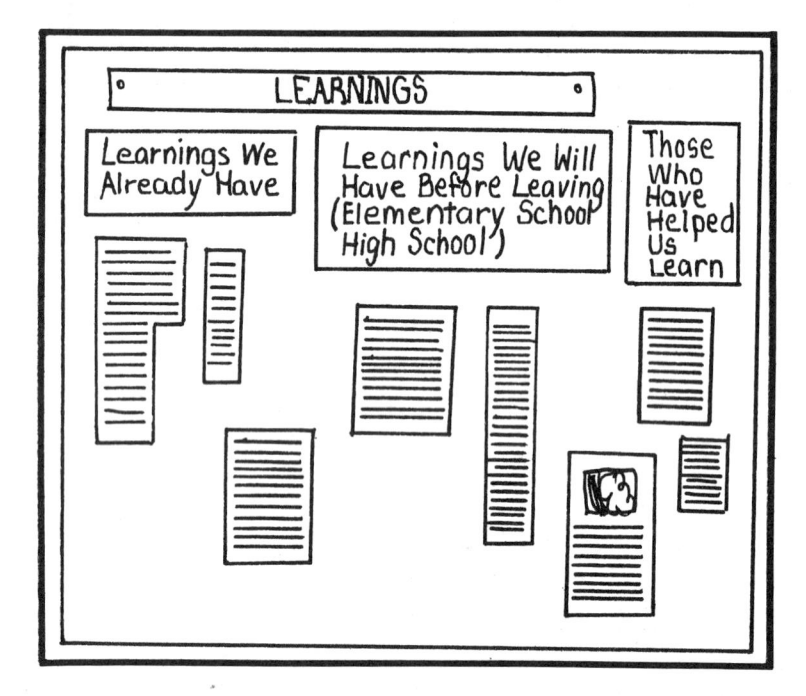

Figure 221

CONCEPTS 141

222 *Learning Inventory*

Conduct a *Learning Inventory* using a form like the one in Figure 222. (Quite likely, many more items are given

(continued p. 143)

Learning Inventory

Learning	Things I can do now	Things I'll be able to do before leaving high school	Learned to do this in: School	Out of School
Tie shoes				
Brush teeth				
Button sweater				
Turn on the TV to the channel I want				
Look up what programs are on TV without any help				
Feed self				
Crawl				
Walk				
Ride a bike				
Ride a skateboard				
Swim				

Figure 222

Learning Inventory

Learning	Things I can do now	Things I'll be able to do before leaving high school	Learned to do this in: School	Out of School
Sit up without any help				
Read				
Kick a ball				
Cross the street by myself				
Work problems such as: 7½ plus 7¾				
Know all of the multiplication tables including the 12's				
Print my name				
Ride a bike				
Drive a car				
Use a telephone without any help				
Go to a grocery store alone and buy something				
Tell time				
Work division problems like: 4428 ÷ 23				

Figure 222 (cont.)

than you would want to use at one time with your own class.)

Follow-up possibilities

1. Discuss the kinds of things learned in school and outside of school. Who have been the teachers for the things that have been learned?
2. Use the Learning Inventory sheets to summarize the common learnings for the classroom members. Which things on the list would we expect a one-year-old to also have learned? a three-year-old? How do their learnings compare to ours? Why is there a difference?
3. Have students administer the inventory to students of different grade levels within the school and summarize the results.

Note

A simplified procedure would be to count the number of items checked and average across a particular grade level, rather than worry about responses to particular items. How do our learnings compare with those at other grade levels? What are some reasons why there might be differences? How do you know that you will have additional learnings as you become older?

223 *Pet Training*

Acquire a classroom pet (rabbit, hamster, rat). As a class, decide one or two things it would be important for the pet to be able to do. Decide on what seems to be the best procedures for bringing about such learnings (feeding right after a desired behavior or gentle talking). Keep track of the days you use the learning procedures and indicate when the learning desired was first observed. How effective were the original learning suggestions?

224 *Learning A New Game*

Have students teach a game (checkers, Flinch, Yahtzee) to other individuals in their class. Afterwards ask the 'teacher' and the 'student' to respond to such questions as:

> How did you help the other person to learn?
> What proof do you have that learning took place?
> What parts of the game were hardest to teach? Why?
> What parts were easiest to teach?
> Why were some parts of the game easier than others to learn?

225 *Teaching Others*

Have your students teach individuals in different grade levels (perhaps kindergarten, third grade, sixth grade) the same game, but one that the 'learners' do not already know. Debrief the experience around such questions as:

> Which groups of students learned how to play the game? How do you know?
> Which group of students learned most quickly how to play the game?
> How can you explain such results?
> What parts of the game were the most difficult for the younger students to understand?
> What explanations do you have for this?
> What knowledge that the learners already had seemed to help the most in learning how to play this game?

226 *Presentation Mode*

Randomly assign your students to one of two groups for purposes of learning from a short crafts lesson. The learning objectives for both groups are the same, but the mode of presentation is to vary. In one presentation mode, lecture and demonstrate how the craft is done. Then have the students do the craft on their own. In the second presentation mode used with the second group, have the students work along with you as you explain and demonstrate how to do the craft. Then have those students build the craft again, but this time without your aid. The student observers are to make the craft on their own. An observation chart like one in Figure 226 might help the students with their evaluative task.

	Everyone	More than half	Less than half	No one
How many students were able to make the craft on their own?				
How many students asked questions while making the on their own?				
Which group seemed to learn more from the lesson?		I	*or*	II

Figure 226

In discussing the final question on the form, have students (participants as well as observers) make guesses concerning why one presentation mode might have been more effective than another (that is, how learning was helped more in one instance than the other).

227 Specialists

Invite persons with various jobs into the classroom and ask them to talk about the special learnings needed in their work. Were the 'special' learnings acquired in school, out of school, or a combination of both?

228 Learner Reinforcements

Draw names to divide the students into two random groups. Use the usual weekly spelling instruction for all students but inform one group that you will give a small prize (such as an M&M candy) for each word spelled correctly on the final test. Involve the class in making general comparisons between the two groups of final tests (for example, compare the number of 100 percents for each group).

Focus questions

    Did you score higher than you ordinarily do?
    If yes, what might be the reasons?
    Did the offer of a prize make you study any harder or longer?
    Do you think offering the prize was a good way to help people learn? Why?
    Do you think offering a prize for learning should be done for most of your school learnings? Why?

229 Learning Logs

Have students maintain short, daily *Learning Logs* for a week. At the end of each week call on several students to summarize several of their learnings for the week and who the teacher was for each learning. The learning log can be as short and simple as the one shown in Figure 229.

Younger students can orally state, rather than write out what they learned for a particular day and who helped them acquire the learning.

CONCEPTS   147

Name _____ Date _____

Today I learned _____

_____

My teacher was _____

_____

Figure 229

☼ **230**   *Teaching A "How-To-Do-It" Lesson*

Allow each student to present to the class a "How-to-Do-It" lesson. Examples can include how to tissue paper an airplane model, how to clean the trucks on a skateboard, how to set a table, how to clean a rabbit cage, how to use an electric drill, how to clean a sink.

After each presentation, involve the class in such questions as:

> What is something you learned?
> What did the person (student teacher) do that was very helpful to you? (e.g., let us try out what she was talking about, answered the questions we had, compared what we were doing to something else I already knew how to do).
> What would you have added to the presentation if this had been your topic?
> Why do you think these changes would have made the presentation even better?

Note

An evaluative guide like the one shown in Figure 230, p. 148, could be employed in this activity.

148 SECTION 2

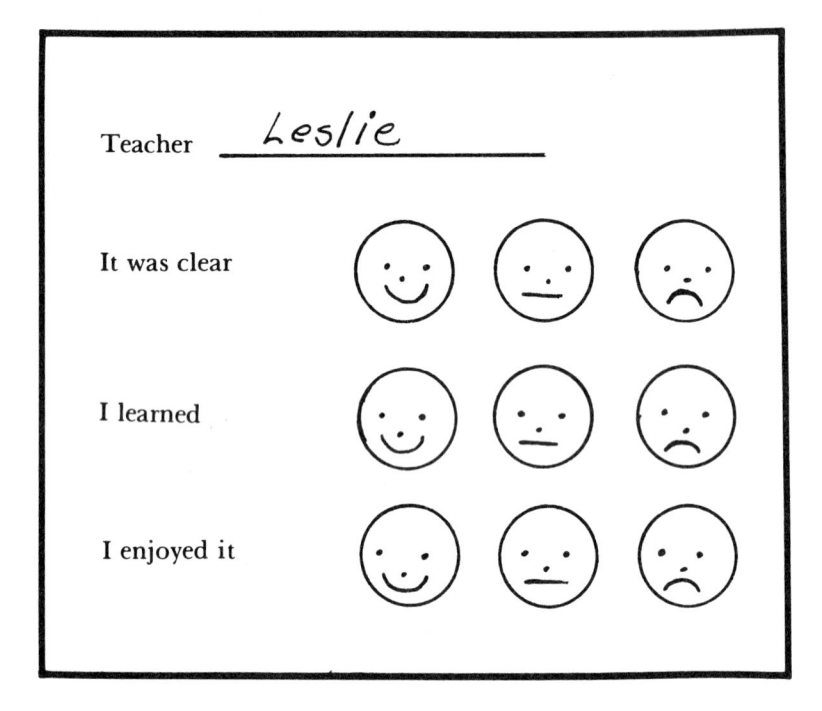

> Teacher *Leslie*
>
> It was clear   😊 😐 ☹️
>
> I learned   😊 😐 ☹️
>
> I enjoyed it 😊 😐 ☹️

Figure 230

231 *The Numbers Game*

Play a simple number game in which a student says a number and you respond with a different number. The procedure is repeated until someone discovers the formula you are following. For example, a series of exchanges might take the following form:

	Number given by student	Your response
a.	3	6
b.	5	8
c.	10	13

Solution: 3 is added to the number given by the student.

The first person to derive a correct solution is then allowed to create a new formula.

Consider interjecting such questions as the following:

What solutions did you try out that did not work?
Who taught you what the right answer was? (Chances are excellent that it was self-discovery).
What are some other times in school when you have to learn things on your own?

Communication

232 *Using Gestures*

Involve the students in demonstrating how gestures are used to communicate.

Possibilities include: a baseball umpire signifying that the runner is out or safe, or that a strike has been called on the batter; a traffic policeman motioning traffic to stop or to pass through an intersection; a football referee indicating that a touchdown was scored, that a team was off sides, or that a time out has been called. Ask the students to consider why spoken words are not ordinarily used in such situations.

233 *Deaf-Blind Communication*

Invite into the classroom a blind or deaf person to discuss the special means they use to communicate and how such communication systems are learned.

234 *Sign Observation*

Have the students begin observing all signs that communicate without the use of words or numbers. Students can draw the signs, share them with the class, and add them to

Figure 234

a bulletin board display. Driver's manuals are a valuable resource for this activity. See Figure 234.

235 *Yes-No Language*

One person selects an object in the class. The rest of the class is allowed to ask a total of twenty questions to discover the object's identity. Only yes-no type questions are allowed. However, rather than orally respond with a *yes* or *no,* the person who made the original selection creates an alternate communication mode. For example, the person might decide that raising the left hand means *yes,* and raising the right hand means *no.* Thus, the question askers must decode the communication system being used as well as ask pertinent questions. Sometimes it is best to have younger children indicate their system to the teacher before starting to use it.

236 *Comic Creations*

Delete the words for a particular comic strip. Have individual students create their own dialogue and then compare their efforts with the original.

237 *Communication in the Past*

Students can research the growth and development of the telegraph, telephone, radio, and TV. Although a report might be carried out on each of these communication advances, interesting alternative perspectivs might also be developed.

For example, the report might revolve around the manner in which election returns were made known to George Washington, Abraham Lincoln, Theodore Roosevelt, and Jimmy Carter. Another perspective is developed if students are asked to report on the various ways people were able to find out about the baseball World Series when it was first played, during the 1930s, and during the 1970s.

Each perspective provides a basis for making many comparative statements regarding the relative speed of communication, the number of people who received the communication, and the amount of detail that was communicated (for example, the TV presentation might be compared to newspaper summaries).

238 *Wordless Communication*

On separate tag-board strips, print the messages shown in Figure 238, p. 152.

SECTION 2

```
"Hello."
"Good-bye."
"I am angry!"
"I like you."
"I don't like it."
"Come here!"
```

Figure 238

Ask volunteers to select a tag-board strip and communicate the message without using words. Each person who correctly guesses the message is given the opportunity to select and wordlessly communicate another message found among the tag strips.

Follow-up questions

What are other messages we sometimes send without using words?

How do we learn to send such messages?

Do you think that persons who do not speak our language would also be able to understand the messages? Why?

239 Creating Ways to Communicate

This activity can get students involved in creating their own methods for communicating without the use of words. Set the situation as follows:

You are involved in a large construction project that requires the use of many pieces of large equipment. You are working with the operator of a very large crane. It is your responsibility to tell the crane operator what is to be moved next and where it is to be placed. However, there is one problem—there is too much noise on the construction site for the crane operator to hear anything you say. Therefore, you must communicate with the crane operator without using words.

Let two students act within the situation, one being the crane operator and the other assuming the role of the person giving directions. Hand the person giving the directions a stack of individual tag-board strips containing messages in Figure 239.

See if the person giving the directions can communicate the messages in the order given to the crane operator. Afterwards ask the observing students to recreate the messages and the activity that was indicated.

Discussion questions

Which messages were the easiest to communicate?
Which were the most difficult? Why?
(Referring to one of the messages, ask: What are other

> "Bring the crane over here."
> "Stop!"
> "Pick up this table."
> "Place the table right here."
> "Well done!"
> "Turn off the engine."

Figure 239

154 SECTION 2

ways this message could have been communicated without the use of words?)

☼ **240**

Have the students close their eyes for several minutes as you continue with a particular lesson. Afterwards, ask what changes in the lesson and the environment would be necessary if the loss of vision were permanent.

Note

Items that would have to be modified or would serve no use include books, bells, clocks, directional signs, and play equipment.

☼ **241** *New-Word Game*

Play the *New-Word* game.
    In this game, you challenge members of the class to think of words that are not listed in the particular edition of the dictionaries found in your room, since the word evolved after the publication date. A variation is to have the student give a 'new' specific meaning for an 'old' word (such as *ZIP*) which might not be listed in the dictionaries available in the room. Depending on the dates of publication, such words as the following might be winners: skateboard, space colony, pot, astronaut, rock, mobile home, moped, CB, solid-state. Follow up with discussion around the idea that words are changing, versus static, entities.

☼ **242** *Art Communication*

Distribute sheets of drawing paper and ask the students to fold them into fourths. They are to use the four divisions of the paper to draw four pictures that show what they

Figure 242

have done so far that day (see Figure 242). The artist is to sign the set of pictures. The drawings are then collected, shuffled, and randomly distributed among the class members. Using the set of pictures just received, each student then reconstructs the events in a classmate's day, using only the data that can be gleaned from the four pictures. Younger students can verbalize such reconstructions, but you may want older students to write a paragraph or two of description. Artists of the 'original' drawings can offer comment on the accuracy of what is interpreted from their drawings.

Follow-up questions

In your opinion, was drawing pictures a good way to let others know what you had done so far today? (Was it accurate? Did enough get told?) Why?

156   SECTION 2

What are the advantages of drawing pictures to tell a story? What are the disadvantages?

What does the use of written and spoken words allow us to do that is not possible if we were to only use pictures?

243   *Coining Terms*

One of the activities suggested for developing the concept *technology,* Activity 260, is to have the students imagine and draw pictures of future technological advances. Besides creating pictures of such technology, the students should also be asked to name their creations. Such a procedure might help students understand that words are coined for new phenomena.

244   *Special Vocabularies*

Involve students in compiling the special vocabulary that becomes associated with various activities. Several examples are listed.

Baseball	*Football*
Grounded out	Down-and-out pattern
Ground-rule double	Buttonhook
Shutout	Reddog
Relief pitcher	Split end
Fungo	Quarterback sneak
Four bagger	Screen pass
Stretch inning	Broken-field running
Grand slam	Split the uprights
Sacrifice	*Citizen band radio*
	10-4
	Smokey Bear

Encourage students to add to the vocabulary lists. You might start a bulletin board display that allows the opportunity for the new words to be added. See Figure 244, p. 157.

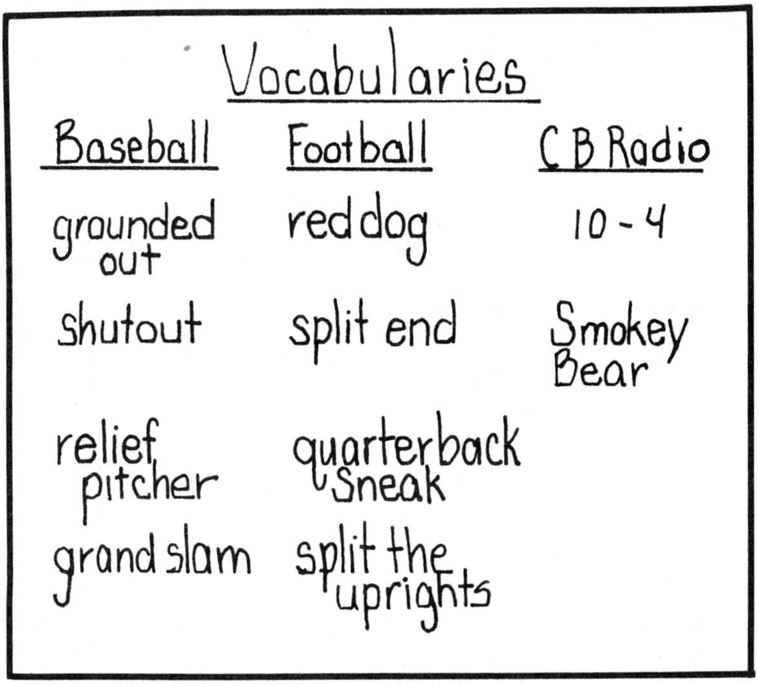

CONCEPTS 157

```
          Vocabularies
  Baseball      Football       C B Radio
  grounded      red dog        10-4
    out
  shutout       split end      Smokey
                               Bear
  relief        quarterback
    pitcher       sneak
  grand slam    split the
                  uprights
```

Figure 244

Follow-up possibilities:

1. Shuffle tag-board strips that contain the vocabulary generated across several activities. Students take turns drawing a tag strip and determine the proper activity category for a particular word or phrase.
2. Divide the class into several teams. Members from each team take turns drawing a tag-board sheet and identifying the word or phrase. A correct response results in one point for that person's team. The first team to score five points wins the game.

245 *Technical Vocabulary*

Tape record a presentation from the radio or TV that contains a heavy usage of technical terms, such as a stock market report. Ask the students to note any words they do not understand. After the recorded presentation, retrieve and list the unknown words.

Follow-up questions

> Why do you suppose that words like those listed on the board are used by people in the stock market rather than words you already know?
> Where are such words learned?

(If possible, relate this lesson to the ideas generated in the preceding activity.)

246 *Meaning Through Intonation*

Through varying intonations the same sentence can take on different meanings. Write a sentence like the following on the board: *I like this.* A volunteer can read the sentence. However, the next person reads the sentence but by emphasizing different words gives the sentence a 'new' meaning. Similarly, another person reads the sentence with an additional meaning. Underlining the words being emphasized can help some students follow the intonation patterns that are used.

> *I* like this.
> I *like* this.
> I like *this.*

Similarly, each of the following sentence types can take on varied meanings through intonation.

> Carl was here.
> Carl was here!
> Carl was here?

CONCEPTS 159

247 The Sentence-Meaning Game

The students can play the *Sentence-Meaning* game.

Write a series of sentences like the ones suggested in Activity 246 on tag strips. (See Figure 247). Divide the students into several teams of about five to eight members each. The play begins with a member of a team selecting one of the strips and reading the sentence on it. Another member of the team reads the same sentence, but through varied intonation communicates a different meaning. The procedure is repeated until no additional and varied communications are generated by the team members. Then the next team selects a sentence strip and begins play. Team points are awarded as follows: 1 point for reading the sentence from the tag strip, 2 points for a varied communication, 3 points for the next variation, etc.

```
┌─────────────────────────────────┐
│  ┌───────────────────────────┐  │
│  │  Ice cream is good!       │  │
│  └───────────────────────────┘  │
│                                 │
│  ┌───────────────────────────┐  │
│  │  Ice cream is good.       │  │
│  └───────────────────────────┘  │
│                                 │
│  ┌───────────────────────────┐  │
│  │  Ice cream is good ?      │  │
│  └───────────────────────────┘  │
└─────────────────────────────────┘
```

Figure 247

160   SECTION 2

Note

It is not necessary that the students be able to read the sentence strips; the initial reading can be done by the teacher.

☼ 248   *Body Language*

Persons also communicate through their body language. Select a topic around which a student might talk freely (such as skateboards, snowmobiles, athletics, a current popular movie, a top-ten recording). As a student speaks on a particular topic, assume such positions as the following:

> arms folded, eyes downcast;
> hands setting on lap, body posed on edge of chair, eye contact established;
> body slouched in chair; eyes closed, head leaning to one side;
> sitting up straight, hands in lap, eyes directed away from the speaker.

For each set of body positions, ask the students to indicate what was being communicated by the listener. See Figure 248, p. 161.

☼ 249   *Listener Response*

As in Activity 248, have one student speak on a topic that is currently popular. A 'listener' is selected and given a card with a 'listener reponse' on it that is to be communicated to the speaker through body movement/ positioning. The remaining students attempt to identify the 'listener response.'

Possibilities for 'listener responses' include:

> "I've heard this before"
> "I have other things I should be doing now"

Figure 248

"I'm really interested in what you're saying"
"I don't have much time for this"
"This is boring"

Technology

250 *Creating Tools*

Create a problem situation in which students must fashion a tool in order to solve the problem. For example, the problem might be to transport several loose crayons across the room and drop them into a jar, without touching them, but using a 6″ × 12″ piece of tag-board provided. See Fig. 250, p. 162. Ask each 'successful' person to explain what he or she did. From the situation, bring out that non-

Figure 250

human life forms tend not to be so creative (e.g., "Have you ever seen a dog or cat make a tool to carry things across the room?").

251 *Creating Tools—Advanced*

After several students have enjoyed success with a simple tool creating activity like the one described in Activity 250, consider increasing the complexity of the task. For example, you might provide a stapler, three small sheets (each about 3″ × 6″) of tag board, and a 20″ length of string to each pair of students in the classroom. (See Figure 251, p. 163.) Then state that the 'work problem' is to use only the materials on hand in order to move six mar-

CONCEPTS 163

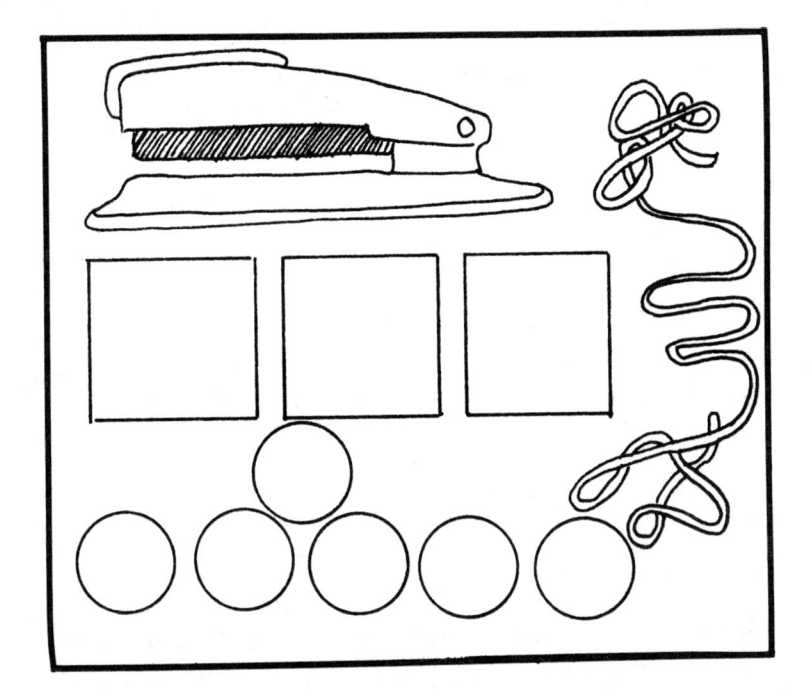

Figure 251

bles at one time across the room with the condition that they cannot be transported by a human being.

After all of the tools have been created, have the students decide on evaluative criteria. Keep the criteria very simple. For example, it might be decided that the best tools are those that most quickly get the work task completed. Thus, each tool use would be timed. Again, in debriefing the activity, emphasize the uniquely human response reflected in their creative activity.

252 *Tool Categories*

Gather all of the tools available in the classroom. Involve students in grouping the tools according to subcategories of *use* (cutting, holding, pounding, etc.), *appearance* (size, weight, color, those made out of wood or metal, etc.). Students could also group the tools according to those needed to perform a specific job *task* (such as tools needed to build a bird cage, tools needed to replace a window pane, etc.).

✻ 253 *Labeling Tool Groupings*

Variation to Activity 252

Arrange the tools into various groupings and ask the students to create several titles for each of the groupings.

✻ 254 *The Tool Grouping Game*

Play a *Tool Grouping* game.

The various subcategories generated from such lessons as these suggested in Activities 252 and 253 are listed under their main headings (such as Appearance, Use, Job to be performed) and displayed before the class. Teams are formed of about six members apiece. A number is assigned to each of the main headings and entered on a small piece of paper (about 2″ × 2″). The numbers are placed in a small box and one of the pieces of paper is randomly drawn, designating the main heading to be used for that turn.

Half of the members of one team leave the room. The remaining members of that team arrange any tools they choose into a grouping that represents one of the subcategories listed for the main heading already drawn. The subcategory is announced to the other students in the room. (See Figure 254, p. 165.) Then the remaining members of the team enter the room and attempt to choose the correct subcategory.

Scoring: 5 points for correctly naming the subcategory on the first guess, 3 points for a correct second guess, and 1 for a correct third guess.

CONCEPTS 165

Figure 254

255 Effects of Technological Change

Ask older students to research and write a report on how changed technology has had consequences for various activities. Help the students with the assignment by stating a specific researchable problem.

Example

Pretend that you must get from New York to Los Angeles as quickly as you can to see your family. Describe how you would do this, or would have done this, for each of the following years: 1900, 1925, 1940, and today. Compare how transportation has changed over the years. When you make these comparisons, see if you can say something about such things as the cost, the time required, and the comfort.

Suggestion

When making an assignment like this one, consider including a year like 2000 in order to have the students predict the futuristic technology in which they will live.

256 Special Tools

Invite into the classroom persons who regularly use certain tools in their daily work (such as carpenter, plumber, housewife, chef, dentist, surgeon, mechanic, a machinist). Ask the visitors to explain how various tools used in their work are operated and how they learned to use these tools.

257 Human Beings as Tool Users

Collect and display pictures of nonhuman beings doing work (for example, beavers building a dam, mother bird bringing food to her young, dog digging in the ground). Discuss what tools might be used by human beings to accomplish the same work.

Alternative

Students could draw pictures of humans doing the same work as the animals and these could be displayed with the pictures of the animals.

Follow-up questions

    What is alike and different about the two sets of pictures?

    What do the pictures show that is special about human behavior?

258 *Tools Inventory*

Have the students conduct a *Tools Inventory* using a form like the one in Figure 258. Students can take the form home and write in the time of day when they used each tool.

Follow-up possibilities

1. Students discuss the various tools they used
2. Ask: How did you learn how to use (name specific tools on the list)? What would you have to do differently if (name a specific tool on the list) were not invented yet?

Tools Inventory

Tool	The Time When I Used the Tool
Knife	
Fork	
Spoon	
Broom	
Dust pan	
Scissors	
Ruler	
Drinking glass	
Bowl	
Plate	
Pan	
Cup	
Ladder	

Figure 258

168　SECTION 2

Consider having students give short dramatizations of how they would try to accomplish a job without the use of one of the listed tools.

☼ 259 *Effects of an Invention*

Identify a specific invention (such as the radio, TV, train, automobile, or airplane). Ask the students to brainstorm the events that must have followed.

Consider using the concentric time circles idea previously described to help the students sequentially organize the events. See Figure 259. Have the students make inferences from the organized data.

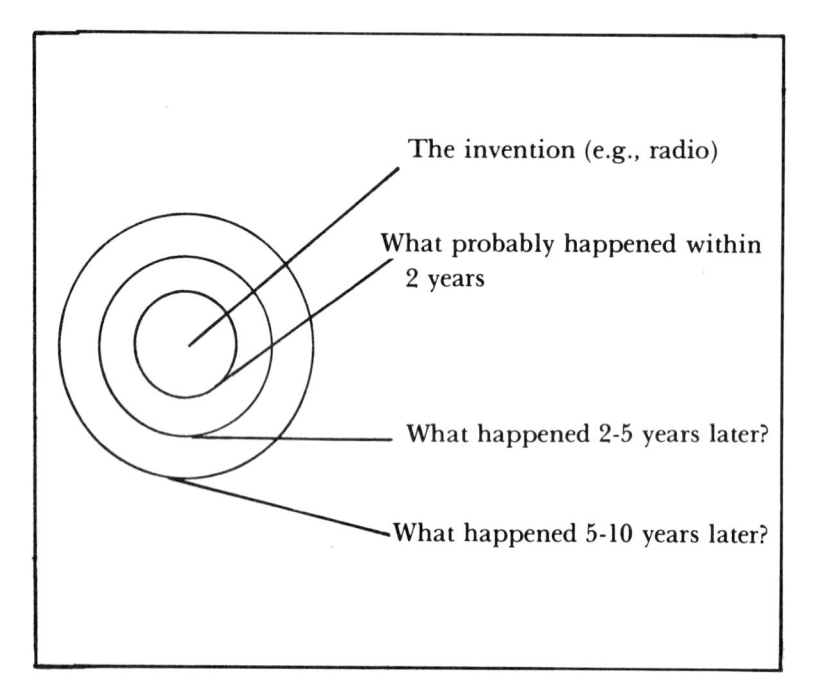

Figure 259

CONCEPTS 169

260 *Future Fantasies*

Ask students to fantasize on what forms future technology might take. For example, pictures might be drawn of vehicles needed in space colonies, future uses of people movers and monorails, automated restaurants and supermarkets, or solar-heated buildings.

261 *Radio-TV Contrasts*

Play a recording of an old radio program (such as Charlie McCarthy, Red Skelton, Fibber McGee). Have the students discuss their impressions of the program:

Was it as much fun as watching TV? Why?
What TV programs now playing are similar to the radio program?
What are the main differences between listening to radio and looking at TV?
What might be the next invention (improvement?) after TV?

Note

See the section on Collecting Original Information for a follow-up possibility in which students interview other people who grew up with radio.

262 *Ad Changes*

Using old magazines, newspapers, and catalogs, have students locate advertising around such topics as air travel, automobiles, and train travel, in order to determine through comparisons with present-day advertising what changes have occurred and the technological improvements leading to such changes.

Section 3

TOPICS OF STUDY

RATIONALE

The changeability of social studies education is best reflected in the topics of study that at any time attract programmatic attention in the schools. Career educaion, consumer education, global education, sexism, and environmental education are all excellent examples of topics that have become significant occupants of the curricular space schools have allocated to social studies instruction.

Topics may be 'in' for a variety of reasons: the ability of individuals and groups of individuals to articulate particular needs; the monetary incentives provided by the government to influence the selection of particular topics for study; and the supportive, concerned interest of society at large. Each of these reasons is constantly vulnerable to shifts in society's perspectives, priorities, and interests; and as a result, specific topics may be revised, changed, or replaced by others.

Rationales and definitions for the individual topics

included in this section may be found in recent social studies textbooks (refer to bibliography that precedes the text in "Using This Book"). However, several comments should be made. First, global education involves the study of the interdependence that exists among the nations and peoples of the world, not the pursuit of globe skills per se, as some teachers have mistakenly interpreted the topic. Also, the topic of *school* has been included, not for any recent swell of support for its inclusion, but rather because of the author's belief that young learners should have the opportunity systematically to study such a dominant activity in their lives. Finally, the topics of study should be considered in conjunction with a study of various concepts such as those introduced in the previous section. For example, the concepts of goods and services relate to a study of consumer education and advertising. Similarly, rules, conflict, learning, and communication all have conceptual applications to a study of schools.

TOPIC: CAREER EDUCATION

Activities

✸ 263 *Personal Interest Inventory*

Ask the students to check off how they feel about doing each of the following activities:

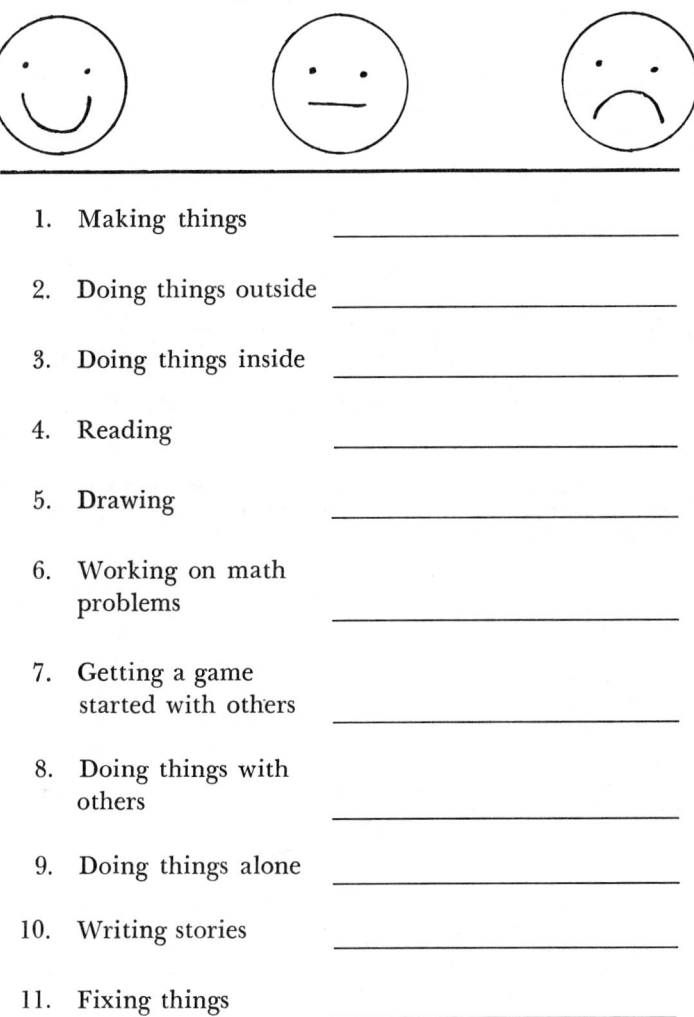

😊	😐	☹️

1. Making things _____
2. Doing things outside _____
3. Doing things inside _____
4. Reading _____
5. Drawing _____
6. Working on math problems _____
7. Getting a game started with others _____
8. Doing things with others _____
9. Doing things alone _____
10. Writing stories _____
11. Fixing things _____

Follow-up activity

Ask the students to refer to their checklist and write (think of, say) several sentences about their interests.

264 *Interest-Job Relationships*

Using the list of interests provided in Activity 263, ask the students to decide which entries seem to go best with various jobs. Consider using the form shown in Figure 264.

Follow-up

1. Have the students discuss their responses with supportive reasons
2. Have the students use the self-inventory completed in Activity 263 and compare it to the assignment of interests to job categories completed in this activity

Job	Interests I have that might go best with the job (Write in the numbers that are in front of the interests you have chosen)
Car mechanic	
Dentist	
House painter	
Gardener	
Bus driver	
Teacher	
Carpenter, plumber, electrician	
Secretary	
Telephone operator	
Delivery person	

Figure 264

Note

The purpose of this procedure is not to get the students to make a career decision, but rather, to begin to perceive some connection between their abilities, desires, and interests, and job selection.

265 *Jobs of Parents*

Where feasible, have a student spend at least a part of a day observing a parent's work routine and environment. Older students might take slide photographs of the work activity and incorporate them into a class presentation. The interview guide offered in Activity 266 could be useful in collecting data for such a presentation.

266 *Worker Interview*

Invite workers into the classroom (e.g., parents, teachers, principal, custodian, cafeteria worker, noon-time supervisors, housewives, superintendent) to tell about their jobs. Consider using the worker interview guide in Figure 266 either before or during the visit.

Worker Interview Guide

What are some of the things you do in your job?
How did you get into this job?
What special training was necessary?
Are there any special tools you use in your job? How did you learn to use them?
What do you like most about your job?
What do you like least about your job?
What are some of the things that we learn and practice in school that are needed for your job?

Figure 266

What are other jobs you think you would also like?
Do you think that men/women (that is, the opposite sex) can/could do your job well? Why?

Figure 266 (cont.)

✲ 267 *Job Positives and Negatives*

Involve the students in drawing up a list of all workers in the school (including teachers, principal, custodian, teacher aides, student teachers, cafeteria workers, noon-time aides, secretaries, bus drivers, visiting teachers, consultants). Invite several of these persons into the classroom or send student interview teams to discuss their jobs. Consider using the worker interview guide presented in Activity 266.

Possible supplementary activity

Ask the visitors what part of their job in dealing with children they find (a) particularly enjoyable and (b) sometimes irritating. As a follow-up procedure, have the class discuss and carry out a plan of action that might reduce or minimize the irritating aspects of a particular school worker's day.

✲ 268 *Employment Classifieds*

Using the classified ads of a local daily newspaper, students might list the various job opportunities. For each job heading (such as salesperson, engineer, mechanic, secretary) the number of jobs advertised could then be tallied.

Follow-up questions

Which jobs are in particular demand?
Which jobs are not mentioned at all?
What are other ways besides using the classified ads to find out about possibilities and vacancies?

Also consider having the students organize the various job headings into such categories as: goods, services; indoor, outdoor; travel, nontravel.

269 *Job Fantasizing*

Ask the students to fantasize about the job they would most want to have and why. Have them draw a picture or write a paragraph that reflects their choice and then share it with the rest of the class. At the conclusion of the activity, the students might be able to offer summary statements about the job fantasies for people in their class (such as most people in our class chose job fantasies that involved sports).

270 *Job Clusters*

Indicate a specific work activity and have the class list all of the different workers involved.

Examples of work activity
Building a house
Treating a sick person in the hospital
Playing a major league baseball game
Teaching school (including teachers, principal, custodians, teacher aides, student teachers, cafeteria workers, noon-time aides, secretaries, nurses, bus drivers, visiting teachers, road guards, librarians).

Alternative

List a particular job and have the students identify all related jobs.

271 *Job Observation*

Assign several students to visit a local business (such as a drug store, grocery store, service station) to observe and list the various jobs involved.

Variation

Ask a student who is to miss school because of a dental or medical appointment to observe and report back on the different jobs being carried out.

✸ 272 *Job Stereotyping*

Distribute a worksheet that includes a list of jobs dominated by one of the sexes. The students can indicate whether men or women ordinarily fill the job and whether members of the other sex might be equally competent. The worksheet might take the form of the example in Figure 272.

Follow-up

Students discuss their responses and the supportive reasons.

Job	Ordinarily this job is filled by a Man/Woman (*Check one for each job*)	In your opinion could/can the other sex do the job as well?
	Man Woman	Yes No
Telephone operator		
Installer of telephones		
Kindergarten teacher		
Doctor		
School custodian		
Cook in the cafeteria		
Pitcher for the Los Angeles Dodgers		

Figure 272

273 Work and Energy Sources

Ask the students to imagine how work is different when the following appliances and items are not available:

>   Automatic washer
>   Automatic clothes dryer
>   Vacuum cleaner
>   Automatic dishwasher
>   Garbage disposal
>   Permanent-press clothes

Consider inviting people into the classroom to tell how work is/was different without these items.

274 Yellow Pages—Jobs

Obtain multiple copies of the Yellow Pages for your community. Assign students to various parts of the Yellow Pages (such as pages 1–5, 6–10, etc.) to list the different kinds of jobs represented.

Follow-up possibility

Organize the various jobs into clusters of related activity (such as medical workers, those who perform a service, those involved in turning out a product).

275 Characterizing Jobs

Embellishment for Activity 274

Have the students list jobs that fall into various categories, such as:

>   Work that involves other adults
>   Work that involves adults and children
>   Work that is done mostly outside
>   Work that is done mostly indoors
>   Work that requires you to fix something

180   SECTION 3

✺ 276   *Jobs Not Listed in the Yellow Pages*

Ask the students to think of jobs that are *not* listed in the Yellow Pages (such as author, professor, teacher, salesperson, professional baseball player). Why are some jobs listed in the Yellow Pages and others not? What added information does this give us about particular jobs?

✺ 277   *Obsolete Work*

Students can compose and present an ad (such as a billboard, poster, radio-TV commercial) for a job that is either obsolete or not as popular as it once was (for example, blacksmith, streetcar conductor, lamplighter, Pony Express driver). See Figure 277.

Figure 277

Follow-up questions

What happened that led to the job's being less important than it once was?

What would have to happen before the job became important again?

278 *Jobs of the Future*

Variation of Activity 277

Plan what new jobs would be required for a space colony.

What jobs that we presently have now would still be needed?

Which jobs that we now have would not be needed in a space colony?

279 *Job Obsolescence and Invention*

What are some things that would have to take place before the following jobs would become obsolete?

>Dentist
>The human teacher
>Fireman
>Letter carrier
>Auto mechanic
>Truck driver
>Custodian

Which of these jobs do you feel has the best chance of being eliminated during your lifetime? Why?

What are several of the related jobs that are eliminated if one of the listed jobs is no longer needed?

What new jobs would be created if one of the listed jobs were no longer needed?

Suggestion

Have the students describe (through pictures or words) how students their age would have a different life if one of the jobs listed above were no longer a necessary part of their life.

280   *Organizational Jobs*

Involve the students in generating a list of the various groups and organizations to which they belong (Scouts, YMCA groups, altar boys, athletic teams, band). Then have them decide for any particular group which jobs are necessary to fill in order for that group to keep going. Which of these jobs require volunteer workers?

281   *Job Hunting for Famous People*

Ask the students to imagine that a famous person from the past is alive today. Have the students predict and give reasons concerning what job that person would probably hold in today's world.

282   *Night Jobs*

Frequently when we think of jobs we think of activity between the hours of 8 AM to 6 PM. Have the students think of night jobs (such as policemen, firemen, custodians, ball park attendants, entertainers).

Follow-up question

How is life probably different in those homes with night workers compared to those with daytime workers?

TOPIC: FUTURE/CHANGE

Activities

283 *Invention Chains*

Students can identify common products in their environment and then determine the *Invention Chain* that has resulted in that product. (Do not be overly concerned if several of the links are missing.)

Examples

AUTOMOBILE: foot ⟶ horse ⟶ horse and buggy ⟶ AUTOMOBILE

ROCKETS: prop planes ⟶ jets ⟶ supersonic jets ⟶ ROCKETS

BALL-POINT PEN: quill ⟶ fountain pen ⟶ BALL-POINT PEN

Follow-up questions

What were some of the advantages of each link of an invention over the link before it?

What were probably some of the disadvantages (loss of jobs, no longer a need for certain skills that individuals had developed)?

Can you imagine how each invention link changed the way people lived from the way it was?

When an invention was introduced, do you think that anyone was against it? Why?

Other possible products for which invention chains could be established:

184 SECTION 3

> Vacuum cleaners
> Automatic garbage disposals
> Light bulbs
> Automatic clothes driers
> Electric shavers
> Typewriters
> Copying machines

☼ 284 *Invention Chains—Creating Links*

This activity builds on Activity 283 involving *Invention Chains*.

Ask the students to create the next link in the chain (for example: What will be the next form of travel after the rocket? Describe how rockets will be used for travel like airplanes are used today). Allow options for these creations (such as written or oral descriptions, drawings, dioramas, skits). Use variations of the questions suggested in Activity 283 for follow-up.

☼ 285 *History Rewrite*

Rewrite sections of history in terms of present-day possibilities.

Example

Settlers moved westward toward California during the middle nineteenth century, spurred on by the discovery of gold. Pretend that it is 1848 again. However, there is one significant difference: Everything that exists today is now also available in 1848. How would the migration to California have been different? (See Figure 285, p. 185).

Figure 285

286 *Scenarios*

Futurists develop scenarios that include their predictions of how things, events, circumstances might someday be. Provide scenario starters for getting your students to consider future possibilities.

Examples

Scenario Starter 1

Grocery stores will be located many miles from the city. Using a computer terminal located in the home, the shopper selects the items wanted, much in the same way as a baseball ticket might be purchased through a ticket outlet. Describe what you think the grocery store might look like and possible ways for delivering what is ordered by the customer.

Scenario Starter 2

Most people will work many miles from where their homes are located. Sometimes the distance from home to work will be as far as 200 miles away and yet the worker will commute each day. Describe the transportation system that would make such a commute possible.

Scenario Starter 3

Almost everyone will retire at the age of forty. Describe what most people will do with the rest of their life.

287 Birth of a Word

Search through a recent edition of a dictionary to find words that were probably not in earlier editions (five years or ten years ago); or, if the word was in the earlier editions, has now acquired additional meanings.

Examples

>ZIP
>Skateboard
>Pot
>Doublespeak
>Aerosol
>Disco
>Rip-off.

By working with several editions, students can estimate when certain words must have arrived and then can make relationships to the societal events of the time.

288 Inventing Names for the Invention

This activity can be related to Activity 287 and to the *Invention Chain,* Activity 283.

For each *projected* link in the invention chain have the students think of a name for their invention.

☼ 289 *"New" Word Game*

This game requires older editions of encyclopedias (a minor problem in most classrooms!). The copyright date of the particular edition is announced. Students take turns predicting topics or words that will not be found in the particular editions being used. One person is designated as the *searcher* (the teacher can assume the role if it facilitates the activity). The searcher indicates whether or not he or she disagrees with the prediction. Disagreements are checked by the searcher. If there is agreement on the prediction, anyone in the class can challenge it (that is, can disagree). The person with the correct prediction becomes (or continues to be) the searcher.

Variation

All players are given ten chips. All procedures are the same except that players bet chips on their positions. The player with the most chips wins. See Figure 289, p. 188.

☼ 290 *Predicting Change*

Study changes that have already taken place and some of the implications of those changes. Then predict a future relatable change and the possible consequences.

Examples

   Change: Permanent-press clothing
   Consequences: Less ironing needed, clothes can be worn for a longer period of time, less work required at home (in ironing), some business at the cleaners might have been lost.
   Future possible change: Wide-scale use of paper clothing

188   SECTION 3

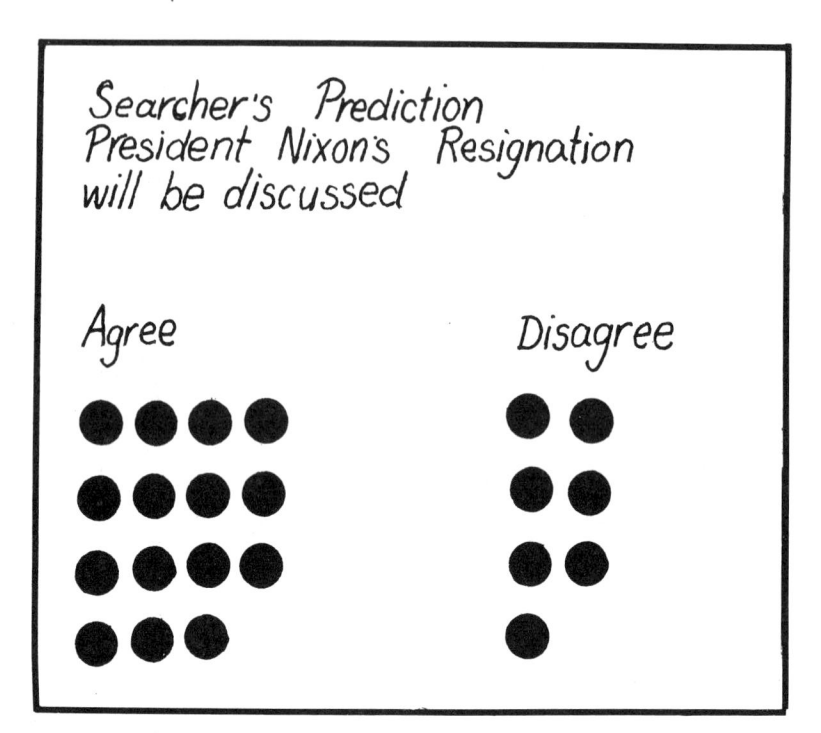

```
Searcher's Prediction
President Nixon's Resignation
will be discussed


Agree                    Disagree

● ● ● ●                   ● ●

● ● ● ●                   ● ●

● ● ● ●                   ● ●

● ● ●                      ●
```

Figure 289

Possible consequences: Less or no need for washing machines and dryers: energy might be saved, less time at home spent in washing and drying chores, might have more variety in what is worn, people who make clothes will probably have to make changes in how they do their job (holding material together, cutting material, packaging), maybe more colors and styles will be available, maybe more people will be able to afford the latest styles, more trees will have to be cut down to make the paper, people now involved in jobs that produce today's clothing materials will lose their jobs.

Change: Invention of the automobile

Consequences: Less need for horses and carriages; therefor, less need for horse feed, blacksmiths, stables and stable employees; need for gasoline stations, paved roads and motels, need for auto mechanics, need to drill for gas and oil, gas and oil processing plants, people can now live further from where they work.

Future possible change: Low cost commuter jets/rapid transit (150 to 200 miles per hour)

Possible consequences: Less need for cars and freeways, might cut down on pollution, might save energy, people might live 100 or more miles from where they work, more pilots will be needed, people might travel greater distances more often than they do now.

Note

In helping students make their predictions, consider using various categories to help them focus their thinking. For example, in predicting the future in terms of transportation changes, consequences might be organized around such topics as: jobs, where people live, new services, new products.

291 *Writing Want Ads*

Students can write job want ads for each of the following positions—all of which will be on a just-completed space colony:

> School teacher
> Carpenter
> Bank worker
> Policeman

Hint

A possible lead-in for this activity would be first to introduce the incentives used to get early settlers to go West and to develop the land.

190   SECTION 3

✻ 292 *Predicting Change*

Have students design, discuss and describe, or draw, the ideal school, home, kitchen, or playground.

✻ 293 *Creating Time Capsules*

Bring in a sufficient number of empty shoe boxes so that each pair of students in your class can use one. Students are to plan together and then place materials in their time capsule (shoe box) that will best indicate to someone opening the capsule fifty years from now what school was like. See Figure 293.

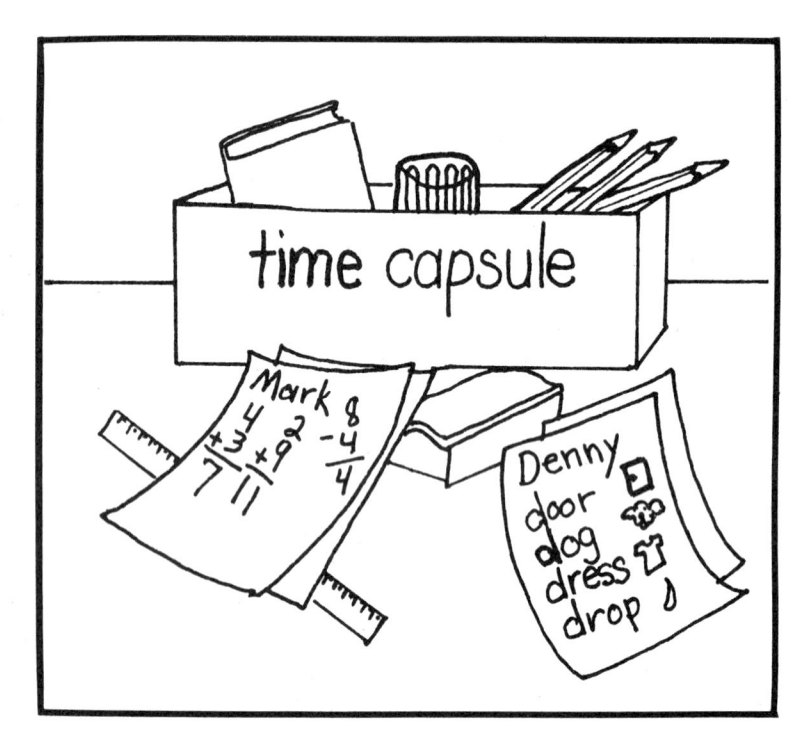

Figure 293

294 Modular Consequences

Presently, we tend to think of a house as a single entity. However, we might also think of a house as a collection of compatible units or modules that might be placed together in varying formations. Have students predict (discuss, draw, role play, construct) how life would be different for individuals if we had large-scale modular housing, modular cars, modular business buildings, modular schools, modular sports stadiums, or modular play areas that with the use of helicopter-cranes could be built or altered in two hours or less.

295 Enjoyable Changes

Survey students, teachers, the principal, or parents on what changes would make life more enjoyable for them. Select several of the responses and decide what creations (products, services, thinking) would be necessary to bring about the sought-after changes.

296 Grandparent's Day

In 1978, a new observance, Grandparent's Day, was established by Congress, to be celebrated on the second Sunday of September. Have the students think of one other new observance they think should be observed, offering reasons for their choices. Presenters might work together and a team of student judges can decide on the best idea.

Follow-up questions

Do you think Grandparent's Day will become as big a tradition as Mother's or Father's Day? Why?

What does it take for something to become a tradition?

297 *Personal Future Changes*

For each of the following ask the students to predict three changes that will take place (a) by the time the present school year is over, (b) by the time they will be old enough to drive a car, (c) by the time they will no longer be living at home: their school, their neighborhood, themselves, outer space.

Follow-up

Have the students fill a time capsule (e.g., shoe box, as in Activity 293) with objects that will reflect what life will be like in the year 2000.

298 *Educated Guesses About the Future*

In the section of this book dealing with thinking processes, educated guesses were introduced. Educated guess questions are especially appropriate for future-oriented instructional activity. Consider using the following educated-guess questions for initiating discussions, art activities, or role-playing activities that require high-level thinking responses:

1. What would happen if we had machines that could record our voice and automatically type out our speech?
2. How would life be different if we had libraries in which the librarian entered a code number for the book you wanted and the book appeared at the desk within ten seconds? (Would more people use libraries? Would people lose their present jobs? Would other jobs be created? Do you think this idea could ever take place? If so, what might the system look like?)
3. How would things be different if people lived to an average age of 150?

4. What changes would take place around us if there were a pill available that would take the place of eating three meals a day?
5. What changes would have to take place if cars, trucks, buses (any motorized vehicle) were not allowed within five miles of our school? (How would teachers, students, cafeteria workers get to school? How would supplies be delivered? Do you think there will ever be such a rule? Why?)

☼ 299 *Prediction Question Box*

After introducing several predicting questions as indicated in Activity 298, set up a *Prediction Question Box*. Students think of and write out prediction questions and deposit them in the box. See Figure 299. A panel of students

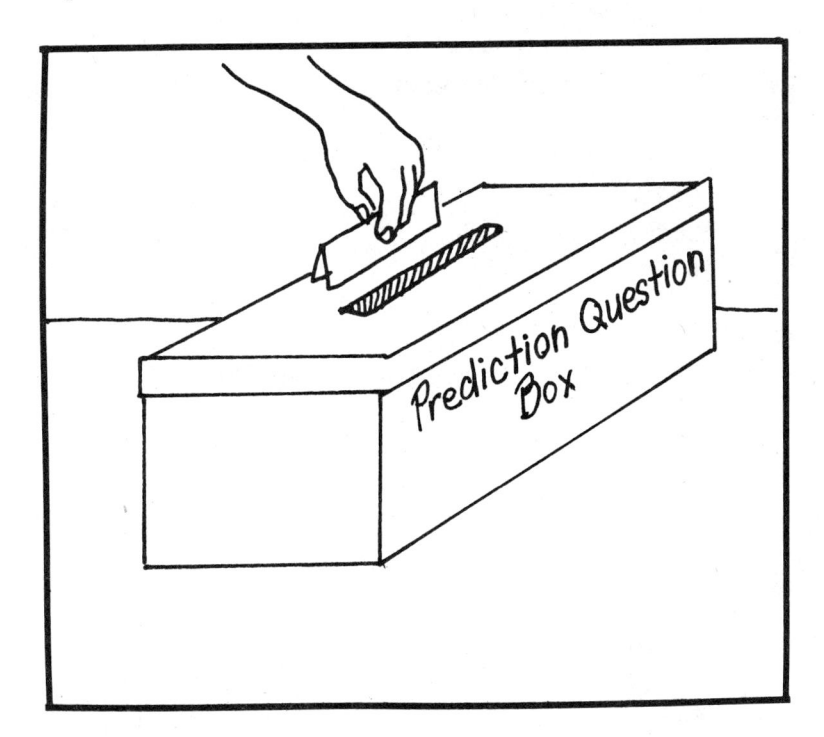

Figure 299

can serve as evaluators and select one question each week for class discussion.

Hint

Introduce prediction questions but allow several days of thought time before conducting a discussion. Such a time delay gives students a chance to discuss the question with other people (parents, brothers, sisters, each other) and to integrate current news events into their thinking.

300 *Picturing the Future*

Have students draw a picture of one thing they will be doing when they are:

1. In high school
2. As old as their parents
3. As old as their grandparents

Quiz students on the reasons for their predictions.

301 *Predicting the Timing of Changes*

Involve students in thinking about possible changes and when they might take place by using a questionnaire like the one in Figure 301, p. 195. Afterwards have the students share and give reasons for their responses.

Variation

Graph the responses and summarize the results.

302 *"Favorite" Changes*

Have students draw one thing they would like to see changed in the world.

TOPICS OF STUDY   195

When I am in high school	When I am the age of my parents	When I am the age of my grandparents	It will not happen during my lifetime	**When Will Each Change Take Place?** *Mark an "X" in one of the boxes for each prediction.*
				1. Most of our food will be harvested from the ocean.
				2. Many people will live in colonies located in outer space.
				3. People movers (like ones found in Disneyland) will be used instead of buses.
				4. There will be no air pollution as we now have it.
				5. There will be no schools.
				6. The weather will be controlled by human beings.
				7. Three-dimensional television.
				8.

Figure 301

Follow-up

What would have to happen in order for 'your' change to take place?

303 *Product Trend Analysis*

Using the advertising found in old catalogs, newspapers, magazines, and brochures, involve the students in a trend analysis of such products as toys, cars, TVs, and radios. Select specific time periods to be included in the analyses according to the materials you have on hand (e.g., perhaps the 1940s, 1950s, 1960s, 1970s). Keep the activity simple by using only a few categories for analyzing the sources, such as size, advertised features. See Figure 303.

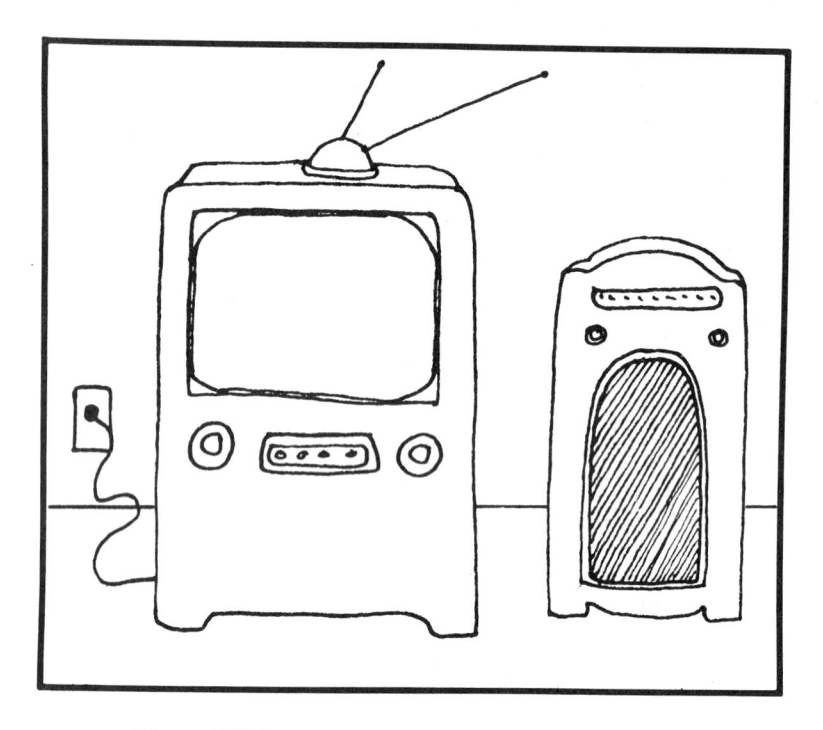

Figure 303

Follow-up questions

How has the product changed over the years? How has it remained the same? In your opinion were the changes for the better? Why?

Predict

What will this product look like when you are finishing high school? as old as your parents? etc.

☼ 304 *Space Plans*

Visit an open space near the school. Have students discuss, draw, and/or create models of the ways they would use the space—if they think it should be put to a different use. Consider having students work together on this project.

Follow-up

Students give reasons for their positions and suggestions.

☼ 305 *Today ⎯⎯⎯⟶*
Tomorrow Changes

Involve students in writing and enacting short skits for each of the following situations as it might occur in the year 2000:

> Taking a family vacation
> A day in school
> Going to the dentist
> Grocery shopping

306 Change and Job Obsolescence

For each of the following jobs, think of possible things that could happen (such as inventions) that would make the job obsolete:

>Grape picker
>Bus driver
>Dentist
>Car mechanic
>Teacher (human)
>Custodian

Follow-up

Which of the things you suggested, or heard others suggest, do you think have the greatest chance of taking place during your lifetime? Why?

307 Making the Modern Convenience Obsolete

What would have to happen before each of the following objects became obsolete:

>Electric shavers
>Lawn mowers
>Clothes driers
>Automobile
>Tires
>Refrigerators
>Soap

Do you think any of these predictions will take place while you are living? Why?

308 Probability and Personal Change

Ask students to make their personal predictions for each of the following:

> How tall will you be when you are fully grown:
> > Shorter than your parents?
> > As tall?
> > Taller?
>
> Where do you think you will live after you are through with school:
> > Where you live now?
> > Not here, but pretty close?
> > Somewhere else?
>
> List three things you are pretty certain you will be doing when you are your parent's age.

Follow-up

For each of your answers print, *R* if you are *really certain* about it, *P* if you are *pretty certain* of it, or *N* if you are *not certain at all*. Ask for volunteers to discuss their responses.

TOPIC: CONSUMER EDUCATION

Activities

☼ 309 *A Class Sales Project*

If possible, secure a donation of a product such as a used bicycle, stove, vacuum cleaner, or lawn mower, that otherwise might be donated to the Goodwill. Involve the class in attempting to sell the product.

Focal questions

How shall we determine the asking price?
    Ask parents what they would be willing to pay for such a product
    Survey the ads in neighborhood newspapers and on bulletin boards at supermarkets
How shall we advertise the product?
    Possibilities include:
    Take out a want ad
    Use bulletin boards in stores
    Word of mouth
    Create and distribute circulars.
Who in our classroom will actually talk with potential buyers?

The 'success' of the pricing and advertising can lead to additional questions:

Are we asking for too much? (if the product is not selling)
Did we ask for too little? (if the product sold immediately).

Other follow-up questions

What did we have to do to compete with other persons selling products like ours?
What seemed to be the most important things we did to help sell this product?

How is what we did like the procedures that department stores, supermarkets, and sporting goods stores also carry out?

How is what we did different from what such stores do?

310 'Best Buys'

As a class, select one product, such as a refrigerator, and launch a search to determine the 'best buy.' Which features seem to be most important? Which features are least important, or at least not as important as others? Involve the students in searches through newspaper ads, brochures, catalogs, consumer guides, and in the collection of recommendations from other people. After collecting data over a period of time, you might conclude the activity by having the students cast a ballot for their selection and then briefly state the reasons for their choices.

Follow-up question

Why didn't everyone agree on the 'best deal'?

311 A Classroom Business Venture

Involve the class in creating a list of inexpensive items that students in your school might be interested in purchasing (such as pencils, erasers, small spiral notebooks, inexpensive pens, paper, paper clips, book jackets). Have the students conduct a school survey to determine which items on the list might generate consumer interest. A form like the one in Figure 311 might be used.

Process the results of the survey and make a final determination of the potential 'best sellers.' Next, determine what the asking prices for the items should be. Such determinations will probably require comparative pricing at local drug stores, variety stores, supermarkets, and dis-

	Would I Buy the Item?		
Item	**Yes**	**Maybe**	**No**
Pencil			
Small notebook			
Pen			
Paper clips			

Figure 311

count stores. Have the students reach consensus concerning what the highest fair price might be for each item.

Consider asking the PTA for a loan of five to ten dollars to finance the purchase of items to be sold at school. Use the results of the previous comparative shopping activity to get the lowest price possible. Decide on the best location within the school for setting up the store and the methods of advertising that would be most appropriate.

After the first day's sale, analyze the results:

What sold best?
What did not sell as well as we had hoped?
What should be done before the next day's sale, such as:
    Raise prices on the best selling items?
    Lower prices on items not selling well?
    Run specials such as: Buy one (hot selling) item and get a (slow moving) item at a reduced cost? Buy two (slow moving items) and receive a discount?

Consider using first day profits and reserves to buy additional items for the next sale.

Analyze again after the second day of sales. Consider using questions like the following:

    After paying back the loan (with interest?) and taking care of all bills, are there any profits?

Are the profits large enough for the time involved?

What did we learn about how prices are set?

Why could we charge more for some items that are priced lower at neighborhood stores and still have buyers?

How long do you think we would be able to do this? Was there enough profit to pay anyone a salary?

What are other expenses we would have to consider if we were to set up our store away from the school building?

How would we try to get these expenses back? How is what we did similar to what happens at a local variety or department store?

Let us compare what sold well for us with the predictions we made after running our presale survey.

312 Neighborhood versus Supermarket

Select several items and particular brands and involve the students in comparing the prices at a neighborhood market and at a supermarket. What are possible reasons for any price differences?

313 Causes of Price Reductions

Involve the students in collecting ads that show how a person can save money by buying in quantity, participating in a clearance sale, or doing something him or herself. (See Figure 313, p. 204.) Discuss the size of such saving and why the seller is willing to reduce prices in each instance.

314 Seasonal Specials

Throughout the year have the students keep track of the seasonal specials (such as around the start of school, near Thanksgiving and Christmas, after the start of a new year, during the Easter season, and around such observances as

```
              SALE
          Men's Jerseys
            $11.99

          (Valued to $21.00)

           Cross Creek
        100% Cotton Lisle
        Long Sleeve Jerseys
          Solids & Soccer Stripes
          Men's Small - X Large

                    19 Central St., Wellesley
                    Phone: 235-2835
                    Open Fri. Eves.
              Olken's
```

Figure 313. (Reprinted by permission of Olken's, Inc., Wellesley, Mass.)

Valentine's Day, Mother's Day, graduation, June weddings). See Figure 314, p. 205. What products/services are emphasized? How do prices change?

☼ 315 *$50.00 Spree*

Distribute $50 in scrip money to each student. Make available several department store catalogs and have individ-

Figure 314. (Reprinted by permission of Olken's, Inc., Wellesley, Mass.)

uals select school clothes. Have several of the students serve as cashiers from whom buyers make purchases, receive change, etc.

Follow-up questions

Why did you choose the particular clothes you bought?
Did you try to have any money left over? Why?
How is this like what your parents must do?

206   SECTION 3

☼ 316 *Washing Machine Purchase*

Present the following situation:

You are interested in buying a new washing machine. How would you decide on three stores you might go to in order to shop for the machine?

Possible follow-up

Supply newspaper ads, Yellow Pages, catalogs, etc., and have the students collect support for shopping at specific places.

☼ 317 *Barter Day*

Set up a *Barter Day* in class. Students bring in two small items apiece they feel they can 'give up.' Each item is labeled with the owner's name and placed on display. After about ten minutes of looking over the display, individuals are allowed fifteen minutes to work out any desired trades with other students.

Follow-up questions

Did you get something you wanted? (If yes: How did you do it?; If no: Why?)

How was it decided what something was worth? What disagreements did you have? Why?

What would it be like if we traded for everything we wanted? Why?

☼ 318 *Salesperson*

Assign to various students the role of a salesperson for a specific make of automobile. For example, different student salespersons might have the responsibility for selling VWs, Fords, or Cadillacs. Give the salespersons a period of days to collect all the information they can for their particular product. Then have other students assume the roles of potential buyers.

Various role identifications might be established, including the following:

> Someone about eighteen years of age who has been saving to buy a car for several years
> A husband and wife who have several children
> A housewife who is shopping for a second car.

Have each of the role-takers visit each of the sales persons. Afterwards, ask the role-takers to make a decision and discuss the reasons for that decision before the class (for example, What did the salesperson say that made the most sense? What problems did they have in reaching a decision?). Similarly, ask the salespersons to discuss the problems they faced and why they chose particular sales pitches for particular customers. Involve the remainder of the class in a discussion of what they would have done in the various role situations they observed.

319 *Toy Trends*

Using recent and older store catalogs, have students list and compare the kinds of toys that are listed.

> Which toys are found in all of the catalogs?
> Which toys (and/or games) have appeared only in the more recent catalogs?
> Which toys from the older catalogs are no longer available? Why might there be some changes in toys that are available? What are possible reasons that some toys keep on selling?

320 *Checkout Counter Items*

Have members of the class generate a list of all of the products they can remember seeing at the checkout coun-

208   SECTION 3

ter of a market. Then have several class members visit a local market, variety store, and drug store and list what is available. Compare the class list with the store's list.

> What kinds of items are found at checkout counters?
> Why might there be an added temptation to buy such products as you are leaving the store?

✺ 321 *Comparison Shopping*

Have the students select a particular item (such as a toy that is a current favorite) and compare the price for that item among several different stores (for example, a local store, large department store, a toy store, a drug store, variety store, discount store, supermarket). What are possible reasons for the best price?

✺ 322 *Consumer Interview*

Arrange with the manager of a supermarket to allow a delegation of students to interview several customers at the detergent shelf on why they are buying a particular product. A simple check list like the one in Figure 322 (p. 209) might be used.

Afterwards, tally the results for the various categories.

Follow-up question

> What inferences can be made from the data collected?

✺ 323 *Product Pricing*

Have students collect comparative cost data for similar products.

Examples

> Convenience and/or prepackaged foods versus the purchase of separate ingredients

Customer Check List

Name of Product Bought	Saw it advertised	Better results	Habit	Price	No particular reason	Other

Figure 322

Store brand versus a name brand

Different forms of food: canned, frozen, chilled, fresh, dried

324 Product Testing

Buy two different brands of the same product and develop tests for deciding which is the better purchase. For example, one group of students bought two brands of artificial logs and decided that the following considerations should be used in a comparative evaluation:

Cost

Weight (lighter the better for ease of transporting)

Ease of lighting (for younger students, the teacher can do this)

Length of burning time

Height of flames

Showing of multiple colors (each package contained claims that several colors would be visible while burning)

Suggestion

Have the students grade each characteristic as *most important, important,* or *least important.* For example, in the preceding example, the students decided that ease of lighting was most important, because of the difficulty of lighting logs outside for campfire use, and that multiple colors was least important. Such distinctions make it easier to reach a conclusion concerning the superior product.

325 *Jingle Testing*

Involve students in formulating ways in which they might test the claims, jingles, and slogans that stores use. Sometimes it takes a while to determine what is meant by such terms or phrases as "You'll like the total better" (What does total equal?); "You won't beat our prices" (prices on what items?); or, "Our service is tops" (What, exactly, is *service*?). Consider interviewing store managers to help develop the specifics of slogans, phrases, and terms. Weekly ads can be followed to check the comparative costs of specific items over a period of several weeks. Definitions of service can be operationalized by comparing the efficiency of check out procedures, the assistance received when trying to locate a specific item, or the accessibility of the store's manager.

Similarly, a refreshment company might claim that even with blindfolds on, consumers will tend to choose its product over a competitor's. Run the same tests in the school and compare the results with those that are advertised.

326 *Cost Reductions*

Have students compare the cost of air travel between two points when certain conditions are met (such as night coach flying, staying at a destination for at least seven days, making reservations well in advance, or group charters).

Follow-up question

What are some possible reasons that the cost decreases as certain conditions are met?

327 Label Reading

Teach students how to read labels. The Food and Drug Administration has developed a new labeling program to help the consumer identify the nutrient content of foods. The format of the label has been standardized, and any food to which a nutrient is added, or which makes a nutritional claim, must have a nutrition label. An excellent description of the new labeling format may be obtained from:

> U.S. Department of Health, Education, and Welfare
> Public Health Service
> Food and Drug Administration
> 5600 Fishers Lane
> Rockville, Maryland 20852.
> Request DHEW Publication No. (FDA) 76-2049.

328 Best Buy Times

Students can guess at when would be the best time of the year to buy certain items and indicate the reasons behind their choices. The answers listed here are taken from *Sylvia Porter's Money Book*.[1]

Item	Good Months To Buy
Bathing suits	After July Fourth, August
Bicycles	January, February, September October, November
New cars	August, September

1. Porter, Sylvia. *Sylvia Porter's Money Book*, Garden City, New York: Doubleday & Company, Inc., 1975. Pp. 146–149.

Item	Good Months To Buy
Children's clothing	July, September, November, December
School clothes	August, October
School supplies	August, October
Skates	March
TV	May, June
Toys	January, February

TOPIC: ADVERTISING

Activities

☼ 329 *Relationship to Viewer Characteristics*

Have students observe the advertising on TV and its relationship to characteristics of the viewing audience. Advertising lists could be generated for such time blocks as the following:

Weekday mornings, before school
Weekday mornings, 9 AM to 12 noon
Weekday afternoons, 12 noon to 3 PM
Weekday afternoons, 3 PM to 6 PM
Weekday evenings, 6 PM to 8:30 PM
Weekday evenings, 8:30 PM to 12 midnight
Saturday mornings

Follow-up activity

Categorize the products/services advertised for each time period and compare categories (for example, How does the advertising for Saturday morning compare to that for weekday evenings? What are possible reasons?)

☼ 330 *News versus Ads*

Obtain multiple copies of the same day's newspaper, or multiple copies of the same issue of a magazine. Students can work in pairs and cut out and separate all advertising and the nonadvertising items.

Various procedures can be used to help the students arrive at some understanding of the proportion of advertising material. One procedure is to draw 3′ × 3′ squares on butcher paper and have the students paste, tape, or staple all of the advertising copy within as many squares as are needed. Similarly, the nonadvertising material is also separately displayed. Statements of comparisons can then be drawn between advertising and nonadvertising space in a particular publication, using 3′ × 3′ (or whatever measurement is used) as a standard unit for comparison.

331 *Nielsen Ratings*

Check the newspaper for the Nielsen ratings for the top twenty TV shows, in terms of share of the viewing audience, for a particular week. List the advertisers for each of the programs. What are various categories these advertisers can be placed into (such as food, services, beverages, cars, etc.)?

332 *Product Presentation*

Ask the students to form into groups of two or three and discuss how they would respond to the following situation:

Three different companies have come to you with three new products:

1. A new brand of sugar-coated cereal that has a free toy in each box
2. A new brand of aspirin
3. A new brand of dog food

Each company wants your recommendation on what time of the day and what kind of a TV program it should consider for advertising its product. What are your suggestions?

Allow several groups to present their different recommendations.

Suggestion

Set up a student panel of representatives from each of the three companies involved and have them decide on the best presentations.

333 *Advertising Copy*

Using a situation similar to the one presented in Activity 332, have students design advertising copy for each product. Display the results and discuss the potential effectiveness of each.

334 *Advertised 'Features'*

Focus on one type of product that is heavily advertised (such as dog and cat food) and have the students bring in all of the advertising they can find on that kind of product. Referring to the collected advertising, involve the students in compiling a list of the advertised features of the various brands.

Example

Dog food

_____ Easy to open
_____ Easy to store
_____ Animals eat it quickly
_____ Animals will look better
_____ Animals will live longer

Then, for each feature have the students place an E before the features for which evidence was presented and an I before those features they feel are the most important. Call on volunteers to make summary statements of the results (such as, "No evidence was offered for any of the claims").

335 Viewing and Reporting

Hint

In carrying out a suggestion as in Activity 334, allow students to bring in what they have viewed on TV. With younger children, you will have to draw the information out. However, older children might be expected to list the salient characteristics of what they viewed.

336 Ads and Self-Worth

Students can be involved in a search for advertising that attempts to appeal to feelings of self-worth. For example, a search might be carried out to find all advertising that hints that 'beautiful people' use a particular service or product. Display and discuss the results.

Other 'self-worth themes' that might be considered include:

"You deserve it"
"Keep up with the Jones's"
"Smart people are doing (or using) it"
"You owe it to others (e.g., in your family, others around you) to do it."

Discuss why such appeals can be effective, especially if we feel inferior or guilty for not taking the advertiser's advice.

337 Disc Jockeys and Ads

Listen to one-half hour of a popular radio program. Use a stop watch to determine the total amount of the half hour devoted to advertising.

Older students can calculate the percentage of advertising in relation to nonadvertising. Comparisons can be made to a one-half hour TV program.

☼ 338   Brand Names

List all of the brand names students can think of when such categories as the following are mentioned:

    Cereal   Tires
    Dolls   Beer
    Games   Cake mix
    Gum   Vitamins
    Aspirin   Movies
    Soap

Follow-up questions

Which brands are the most popular for each category?

Which brands have you heard of on the TV or radio? (Discuss how much of the information has come from these sources.)

Why do you think you have remembered these specific brands? (such as a catchy jingle, a celebrity makes the endorsement, a funny presentation, etc.)

Would you say the advertiser has been successful in getting you to remember a particular brand? Why?

Why is this important to the advertiser?

☼ 339   Name Repetition

Tape record a segment of advertising from the radio or TV. Have the students tally the number of times the name of a particular product or service is given. Discuss possible reasons concerning why the name is presented repeatedly.

☼ 340   Roman Chariot Ads

Students can create TV ads and skits to sell pre-TV/radio items, such as Roman chariots, printing presses, early models of bicycles, excursions on clipper ships, cave furniture, and all-purpose wooden clubs used by cave people.

341 Foreign Ads

Check out foreign magazines (such as *der Stern,* from Germany) from a local library. Have the students identify all ads for products sold in the United States (such as Kodak, Alka-Seltzer, various brands of cigarettes, cola drinks).

Variation

Before the search for the ads, have the students predict which products sold in America might be advertised in the foreign magazine.

342 Ads and Children

List specific children's programs. Ask the children to list orally or in written form who advertises on each of the programs.
   Ask:

Why do you remember these products?
Why is this of importance to the advertiser?

343 Creating Effective Ads

Have individual students, or groups of students, create ads (posters, tapes, displays) for an identical product. Place all of the results on display. Invite students from another class to review the ads and vote for their favorite ad. The results can then be tallied and the winners determined. Individuals from the visiting class might then be invited back in order to discuss their reasons for particular selections.

344 Ads for Special Audiences

This activity is a good follow-up to Activity 343. Ads are created for the same product/service by individuals or groups, but with two different audiences in mind (such as a first-grade class and a sixth-grade class). All ads are placed on common display and each of the two different classes has its own viewing period. Voting on the favorites is summarized and compared between classes.

Follow-up questions

How were the selections alike/different between the two classes?

What are possible reasons for these results?

Did the ads created for certain classes seem to work? Why?

345 Creating Classified Ads

As a class, write a two-line classified ad for a three-speed bike. (Consider calling a newspaper for the number of words allowed for two lines.) What features should be pointed out? If possible, work with someone willing to donate a bike, then place the ad, and attempt the sale.

346 Features Analysis

Secure magazines, catalogs, or newspapers several years old. Have the students select one product category (such as toys, cars, kitchen appliances) and compare the features that were highlighted several years ago with present emphases.

347 Ads of the Future

Create an ad for air travel across the United States in the year 2000. Do the same thing for ground travel.

348 *Ad Categories*

Collect ads and randomly display them on a bulletin board. Then involve the students in rearranging the ads according to various categories.

Examples of categories:

Products, services
Food, appliances, cars, banks, entertainment
Basic needs: food, clothing, shelter; nonbasic needs
Small purchases, large purchases
Things that require additional use of natural resources in order to be used (such as automobiles)

349 *Buying From the Ads*

In this activity, students pretend they are going to buy a certain product (such as a washing machine). They are to state and list the most important features to look for in making such a purchase. During the subsequent week, they collect all the available advertising for the various product brands.

Follow-up questions

Which ads contain information on the features we thought were most important?
Which of the ads are most helpful? Why?
Which ads did you like the best? Why?
Which brand would you buy?
What are your reasons?

350 *Nonradio/TV Advertising*

Cigarette and hard liquor advertising are not allowed on TV or radio. Students can survey what other advertising media are used as alternatives (such as sponsorship of a golf or tennis tournament, billboards).

351 *My Favorite Ad*

Involve the students in selecting their favorite advertisements on TV and the reasons for their selections.

Possible follow-up questions

What is there about the ad that you especially like? (a jingle? the characters involved? the music?)

Do you also like the program that has this advertisement?

Do you think that this is important? Why?

How might the people who write advertising find out what boys and girls like?

Do any of the ads suggest that you tell your parents about a certain product? Which ones? (Help the students see that there are indirect ways to accomplish this.)

Sometimes parents have complained about the advertising on children's programs. What would you guess they were complaining about? Why might companies advertise on children's programs even though they know that adults, not children, are the ones who will probably do the buying?

352 *Product Recognition*

Visit a store and list all of the brand names within a particular section (such as cereals, vitamins, or bread). Involve the students in identifying the brand names they have heard of through advertising. A dittoed handout like the one shown in Figure 352 (p. 222) might be helpful here.

Focus questions

What can you say about the product?
Where did you get this information?
Is the information useful? Why?

List of All Cereals Found in Big Orange Market

	Is It Advertised?	
	Yes	No
Brand A	___	___
B	___	___
C	___	___

Figure 352

353 *Ad Homework*

Hint

Activity 352 might be carried out during school time. However, also consider the activity as a possible homework assignment.

354 *Box-Top Patterns*

Have students bring in the top for any cereal box that is used in their house during the week. The tops are then grouped according to brand names and displayed on the bulletin board.

Focus questions

    Using the display, what can you say about the cereals used by people in the class during the past week?

    Which of these products are advertised? Where? When? How often? (If possible, determine which brands are advertised the most.)

    Did any of you help decide on the particular brand you brought in?

    Do you think there might be any connection between

what you suggested to your parents and the advertising you heard and saw? Why?

355 *School Activity Ads*

Plan and carry out the best ways to advertise such school events as the following:

> A PTA meeting
> Open house
> A class program
> An antilitter campaign
> A newspaper drive
> A school yearbook sale

356 *Issue Focused Ads*

After discussing a controversial issue (such as a proposed freeway that would require the removal of existing housing; proposed dog leash laws; rationing gasoline/water/heating oil), students can create a one-page newspaper ad that reflects their position and at the same time might influence the opinions of other people.

357 *School Environment Ads*

Discuss a change at school that would lead to a more positive school environment (perhaps in the halls, classrooms, cafeteria, or playground). Plan and launch an advertising campaign to bring about the desired changes.

358 *Ad Results*

An added suggestion when implementing Activity 357 with older children:

Collect observational data around the desired change (such as a quieter cafeteria) before and after the advertising campaign begins.

❂ 359 *Selling Nature*

Have the class discuss the problems of promoting the sale of a natural product (such as oranges, apples, drinking water).

What characteristics might be highlighted?
Do any of these characteristics really make a difference? Why?

Collect appropriate ads to observe the direction taken by various companies in their advertising.

❂ 360 *Selling the Similar*

This activity has a similar theme to Activity 359.

Different airline companies might charge identical fares between the same cities. Compare ads among the competing carriers and identify what is highlighted as important when the fares are the same. What evidence is offered for any claims for superior service?

❂ 361 *Ads and Personalities*

Locate ads that include actors, actresses, and athletes. Why are such people included in ads? Select the ads in which these famous people are making statements that have little to do with their job as performers.

❂ 362 *Classified Ads Game*

Involve the students in the *Classified Ads Game*.
On separate index cards, list items that might be available through the classified ads.

Examples

    1975 VW sedan
    Three-bedroom home in (list a specific section of town)
    Secretarial job
    A lost dog
    1977 Cadillac
    House painters
    Outboard motor—10 h.p.
    Ten-speed bike
    Motorhome
    Moped
    Kitten
    Firewood
    A job as a salesperson

Have a student draw a card and then search the classified ads of a local newspaper for the item indicated. This activity can be turned into a game with teams awarded points for being the first to furnish specific usable leads.

363 *Job Ads*

Have the students make a list of the different job types/categories advertised in the newspaper.

Follow-up questions

    What are some jobs that never seem to appear in the ads?
    Guess at why these jobs are ordinarily not advertised in the paper.
    How do persons probably learn of the job possibilities that are not advertised in the paper?

364 *Historical Ads*

Select an event in history and write an advertisement that might have been used at the time.

Examples

1. Guards needed after the Boston Tea Party to protect English trading ships.
2. Columbus recruiting men for a voyage to the West Indies.
3. Meeting to be held to discuss the injustice of being taxed without representation.
4. Soldiers needed by the South during the War between the States.

For most students, the advertisement will probably take the form of a poster. However, some students might bring the event into the twentieth century and create ads that would be suitable for TV or radio presentation.

365 *Publicizing A Favorite Book*

Have the students create a newspaper ad for their favorite book. Display all ads. Involve the students in a discussion of their favorite ads and any connection with wanting to read a particular book.

Note

This procedure is especially effective in interesting students in a variety of library offerings.

366 *The Sixty-Second Sales Pitch*

Small groups of students can work together to create a sixty-second sales pitch for a particular book. Presentations can be made to a panel of students who decide on the best presentations. Panel members give specific reasons for their selections. The students involved in the presentations are given the opportunity to discuss how they decided what to highlight during the sixty seconds allowed.

367 Sixty-Second Analysis

Follow-up to Activity 366

Record an ad from TV or radio that takes about sixty seconds or less. Compare these ads with the ones presented in class. For example, how many times was the product's name mentioned? Was a jingle or song used? Was more than one person included in the ad? Was there a dramatization?

368 'Bait and Switch'

Invite a representative of the local Better Business Bureau into the classroom to discuss deceptive practices sometimes used in advertising (such as 'bait and switch' or monthly payments that fail to mention the balloon payments at the end) and how these practices can be detected.

369 Advice on Ads

Write a letter to a TV or radio program commenting on their advertising (for example, Why the ads are 'good,' 'poor,' need evidence for claims, take too much of the program's time, etc.).

370 Animal Ads

Dogs and cats do not buy food and flea collars—their owners do. Analyze how advertisers get their messages across to the owner and yet sometimes seem to be conversing with the animals.

371 Selling the Obsolete

Involve the students in writing ads for a product that is no longer generally used. See Figure 371, p. 228.

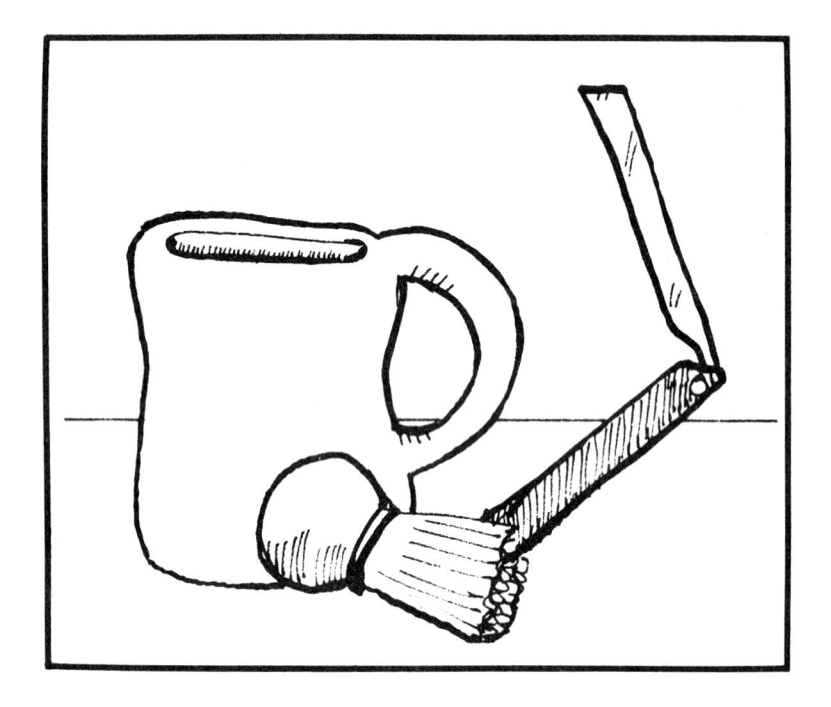

Figure 371

Examples:

> Straight-edge razors
> Shaving mugs and brushes
> Ink blotters
> Fountain pens

Follow-up questions and activity

What 'present day' desires/needs of people did you draw on to sell your product?
Did you try to make the listeners feel guilty if they did not have your product?

Locate examples of advertising in which a product is not vital, or maybe even functional, yet is presented as a worthwhile purchase (such as racing stripes on the family car, decorator telephones).

TOPIC: GLOBAL EDUCATION

Activities

372 Classroom Inventory

Inventory and list all foreign-made products found in the classroom, including games, tools, and toys.

373 Foreign Product Inventory

Have students check for all items they presently have with them that are foreign made. Younger students will need assistance in reading clothing labels, watch manufacturers, etc. Older children can locate and mark the foreign countries on maps and seek relationships between various countries and the manufacturing of specific products.

374 Roots

Call on students to identify one country that represents their ancestral background. On a map, draw a line or pin yarn from that country to your location in the United States.

> What inferences can be made?
> For example, Are the ancestral patterns mostly African? Asian? European? American?

375 Foreign Products at Home

Students can inventory all foreign-made products at home. Possibilities include TVs, radios, cars, toys, games, automobile tires, and foods. List all items and place them into categories. Ask the students to make statements concerning the categories of foreign products found in their homes.

230   SECTION 3

☼ 376 *Foreign Businesses*

Have students search the telephone Yellow Pages and list all businesses that rely in some way on a foreign country for their operation, either partially or totally.
    Possibilities include:

>   Banks
>   Appliance Stores
>   Restaurants
>   Travel agencies
>   Airlines
>   Certain schools.

☼ 377 *Foreign versus Home News*

Using the first pages of the front section of a metropolitan newspaper, cut out all articles and place them into one of two groups:

News that has a United States dateline
News that has originated outside of the United States

Follow-up possibilities

1. Locate the origin of each news article on a map.
   Where was the news concentration for this particular newspaper edition?
   Where did most of the foreign news come from?
   From which cities within the United States did most of the domestic news come?
   Suggestion: Have students first guess the answers before looking at the articles.
2. Cut all of the news articles from both groups (United States and outside of the United States) into some agreed on standardized size (such as the width of one news column times two inches). Count the total number of standardized sizes for each stack of articles and make comparative statements.

378   Bicycle Survey Study

Survey the number of foreign cars and bikes found in a nearby parking lot or that pass by the school during a fifteen to thirty minute period of time. Someone can count all of the cars and bikes and someone else can count the foreign models. Younger students can work with older ones in making identifications and in recording the data. For easier data interpretation, translate the data into a graph that can be easily seen by everyone in the room (see Figure 378, p. 232).

Focus questions include

> What does the graph show?
> Do you think this is the way it is everywhere in the United States or just in our neighborhood?
> Do you think we would get the same results if we made observations again? Why?
> How can we check out our guesses?

Hint

An embellishment to Activity 378 might include categorizing all of the observed cars as either United States or foreign and standard size or compact. Analysis of such observations could help the student more specifically pinpoint the impact of foreign cars on the United States market.

379   Supermarket Imports

Choose one section of a grocery store and survey the products imported from another country.

Follow-up questions

> For a particular product, how many of the brands are from the United States and how many come from another country? *(cont. p. 233)*

232   SECTION 3

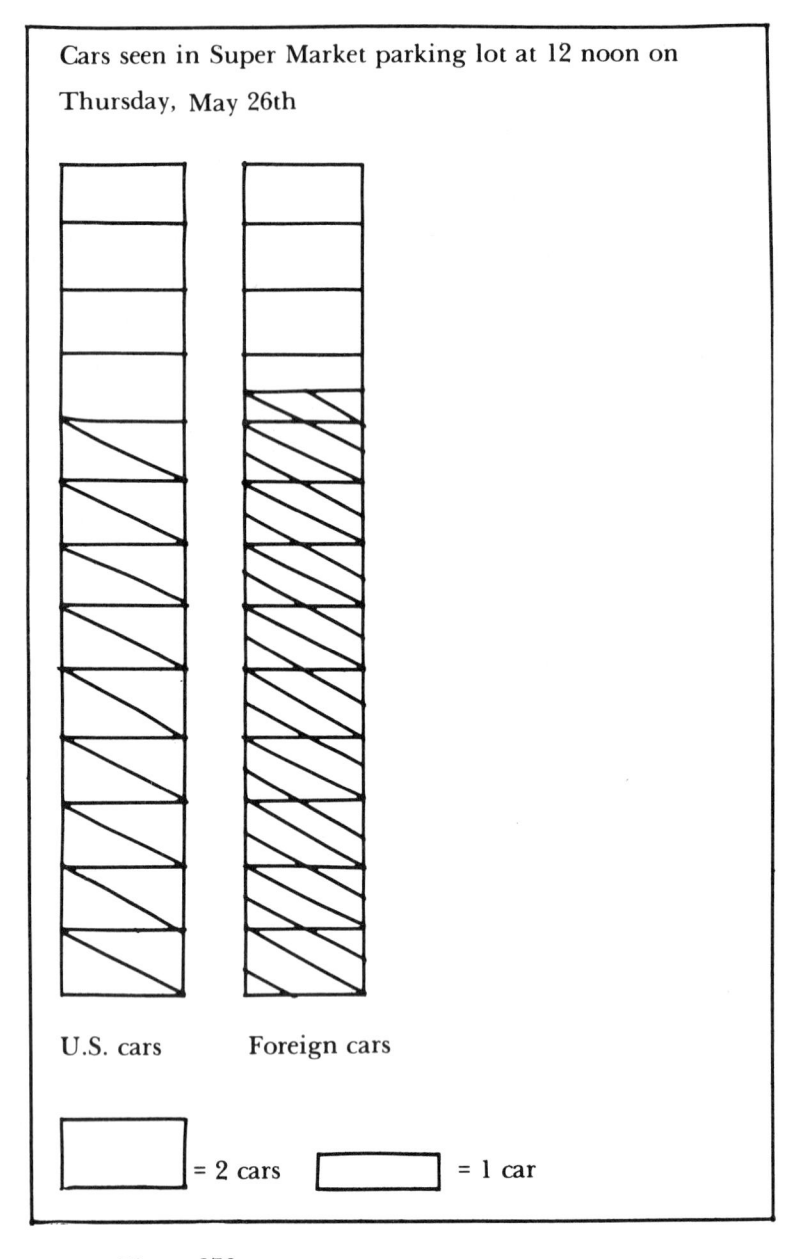

Cars seen in Super Market parking lot at 12 noon on Thursday, May 26th

U.S. cars   Foreign cars

☐ = 2 cars   ☐ = 1 car

Figure 378

Compare and make a statement about the prices of United states and foreign imports.

Which of the kinds of products surveyed had no foreign imports?

Why might this be so?

Which of the products surveyed had the most foreign imports?

Why do you think this might be so?

380 *Neighborhood Business Survey*

Conduct a field trip through your neighborhood for purposes of identifying any businesses that rely to any extent on imported products.

Examples

> A foreign car repair
> A Mexican restaurant
> A bike shop that includes foreign makes

Take pictures of each establishment and involve the students in creating a display for the classroom.

381 *International Symbols*

Introduce signs and symbols that have meanings across cultures. (See Figure 381, p. 234.)

Examples

> Musical notes
> Symbols in chemistry
> Friendly gestures

382 *Foreign Trip*

Involve the students in planning a trip from their city to a foreign country. Draw out from the students which coun-

234   SECTION 3

Figure 381

tries are involved in supplying the necessary transportation.

✱ 383 *Letter Exchange*

Survey the class to determine who has relatives or friends in another country with whom communication is still carried on. Such contacts could lead to letter exchanges between class members and students of the same age living in another country.

Possibility

Have the students find out what school is like for the foreign student, how weekends are spent, etc., and compare the data to life in the United States.

384 Port Schedules

Have someone report the schedule found in many newspapers of the daily/weekly ship arrivals and departures for a nearby port, including the cargo and the cities of origin and destination. Display a world map and place pins on the locations of the cities involved in these port activities.

Note

Consider the pins as data points from which the students can make statements concerning the relationships between the designed cities.

385 Exchange Students

Contact the foreign student organization of a local college or the representative of a student exchange program within your school district. Request that a foreign student visit your class to discuss their impressions of life in the United States and how it compares with their own country.

386 Interviewing A Foreign-Born Person

Have a group of two or three students interview a person who was born and raised in a foreign country, but who now lives in the United States. The interview could occur in a small group setting or before the entire class. Consider having the students use an interview guide like the one in Figure 386.

Note

With some modifications, this interview would also be appropriate for use in Activity 385.

Interview Guide

My name _____

Name of the person interviewed _____

Date of interview _____

Questions	Answers
What country did you live in before coming to the United States?	
What are some things you noticed right away about the United States?	
How is the United States most like the country you came from?	
How is the United States most different from the country you came from?	
What do you like most about living in the United States?	
What have you missed most since coming to the United States?	
What were some of the changes you have had to make since moving to the United States?	

Figure 386

TOPIC: SCHOOL

Activities

✣ **387** *School Jobs*

Involve the students in brainstorming a list of all the jobs needed to keep a school functioning. At first, students will probably identify the jobs conducted at the school site (teacher, principal, cafeteria workers, custodians, secretaries, nurse, visiting teachers, parent helpers, school crossing guards, etc.).

However, then have them consider jobs that are ordinarily conducted away from their school, but that are necessary for the school's operation (such as superintendent, consulting teachers, district physicians, district library personnel, delivery truck drivers, etc.).

Possible follow-up questions

Which jobs go together? (that is, name the categories). Make a statement about the jobs that are needed to keep a school going.

✣ **388** *Interdependence Wheel*

An extension of Activity 387 is to use an *Interdependence Wheel* to help the students understand the interrelationships among the jobs and functions required to run a school. Start with the *Student* as the hub of the wheel and develop the support personnel and functions from here. See Figure 388a, p. 238.

Consider duplicating this scheme and having small groups of students work together to identify specific jobs (including the names of specific individuals holding the jobs, whenever possible). This activity might entail observations, interviews (including phone interviews) and visits to other sites. Of course, the detail of the spokes of

238   SECTION 3

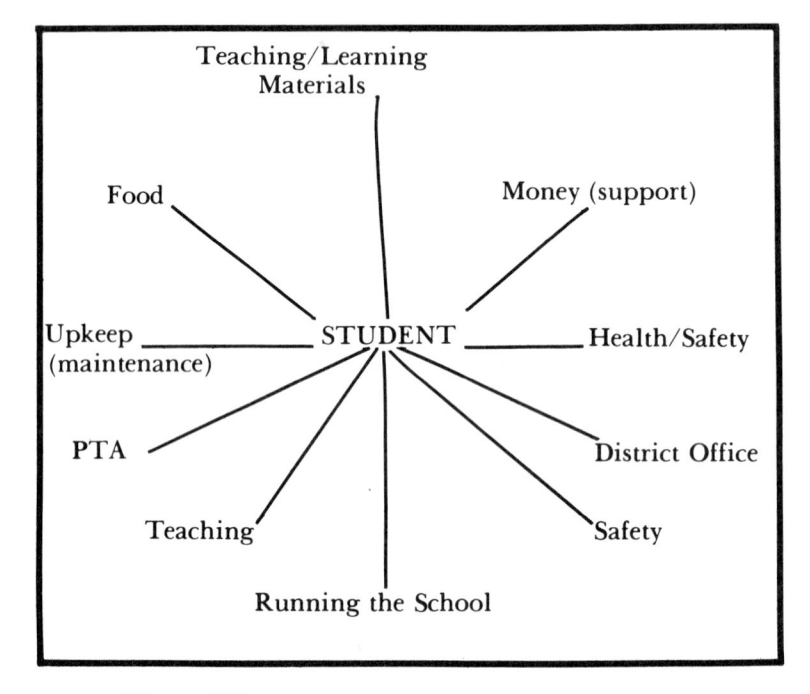

```
                 Teaching/Learning
                     Materials
        Food                          Money (support)

Upkeep _____ STUDENT _____ Health/Safety
(maintenance)

    PTA                                 District Office

       Teaching                      Safety
                 Running the School
```

Figure 388a

the wheel will vary among different groups of students, as will the time devoted to the activity. Several possible developments for several of the spokes are shown in Figure 388b, p. 239.

Regardless of the detail worked out, have the students reflect on what they have learned from this activity through such questions as the following:

How many different kinds of jobs did we name that are needed to run a school?
What did you learn about running a school that you did not know before your involvement in this activity?

✵ 389 *Using the Wheel*

Consider displaying an *Interdependence Wheel* like the one described in Activity 388.

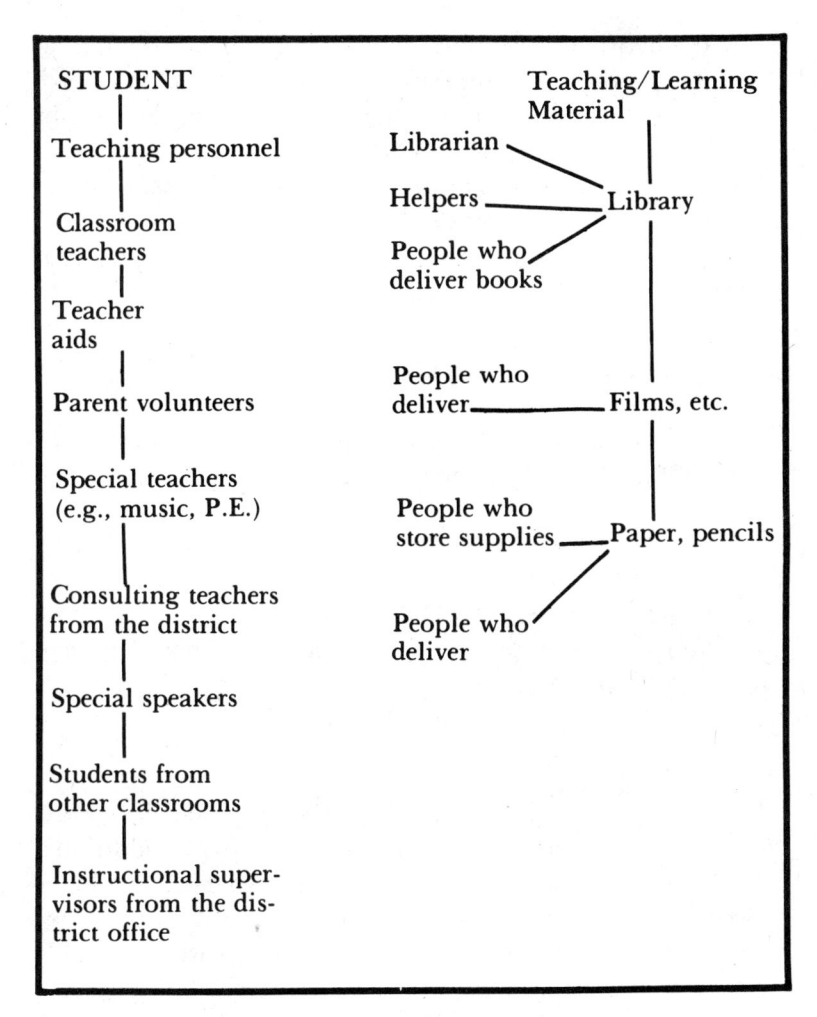

```
STUDENT                          Teaching/Learning
  |                              Material
Teaching personnel      Librarian       |
  |                        |            |
Classroom               Helpers_____Library
teachers                   |       /
  |                     People who/
Teacher                 deliver books
aids
  |                     People who
Parent volunteers       deliver_____Films, etc.
  |
Special teachers
(e.g., music, P.E.)     People who
  |                     store supplies___Paper, pencils
Consulting teachers                   /
from the district       People who  /
  |                     deliver
Special speakers
  |
Students from
other classrooms
  |
Instructional super-
visors from the dis-
trict office
```

Figure 388b

During the school year, refer the students to the wheel and determine where various classroom visitors might fit in. For example, many teachers will be visited by a supervisor from the district office during an instructional period and miss an opportunity to tell the students (at least afterwards) who the visitor was as well as his or her function. Similarly, a student may be asked to assist another student in learning a list of spelling words or in figuring out a mathematical application. Thus, the student is serving, at least temporarily, a teaching function and fits on one of the wheel's spokes. On another occasion, a student might help out in the school cafeteria, or serve as a crossing guard. By referring to an *Interdependence Wheel* showing school activity, the students can be assisted in learning how various jobs are directly involved in the running of the school.

390 School-Job Interdependence

Ask students to discuss how things would be different for them if any of the following events were to occur:

- The regular classroom teachers did not come to school (for example, a strike was called)
- Property owners refused to pay their taxes
- All special teacher jobs (such as the music teacher) were eliminated
- The custodians would be able to come to the school only once a week
- All of the buses broke down

Students could be called on to provide additional situations. Have students predict what changes would be required at school if persons were not available to carry out certain jobs. For example, if custodians were available only once a week, then students and teachers might have to do much of the cleaning the other four days of the week —or at least be more careful about trash than they had been.

In extending this activity, it might be helpful to have the students develop their cause-effect predictions and suggestions by using a chart like that in Figure 390, p. 241.

Referring to the chart, students can then generate a list of alternatives if certain changes were to occur. For example, cut-backs in custodial help lead to various possibilities:

Job description	Results of the job	Who ordinarily does the job
Sweep, dust, scrub floors, pick up	A clean classroom	Custodian(s)
Road crossing guard		
Principal		
Teachers		

Figure 390

1. Maintain the results of the job, but find someone else (students? teachers?) to carry out the job tasks
2. Give up the results of the job by not replacing the custodians
3. Expect less—have custodians at school just one day a week

☼ 391 *School Subjects Questionnaire*

Research the subject preferences of students, using simple questionnaires like the one shown in Figure 391.

Hints

1. Use few rather than many categories, or the data will become too cumbersome for the students to interpret.
2. Consider the following options for collecting data with younger students:
Have the students close their eyes and you read the questionnaire to them. Record how many students raise their hands for each face per subject category.

242   SECTION 3

**How I Usually Feel When It is Time
For Each of These Subjects**

Mark an X through one of the faces in each row.

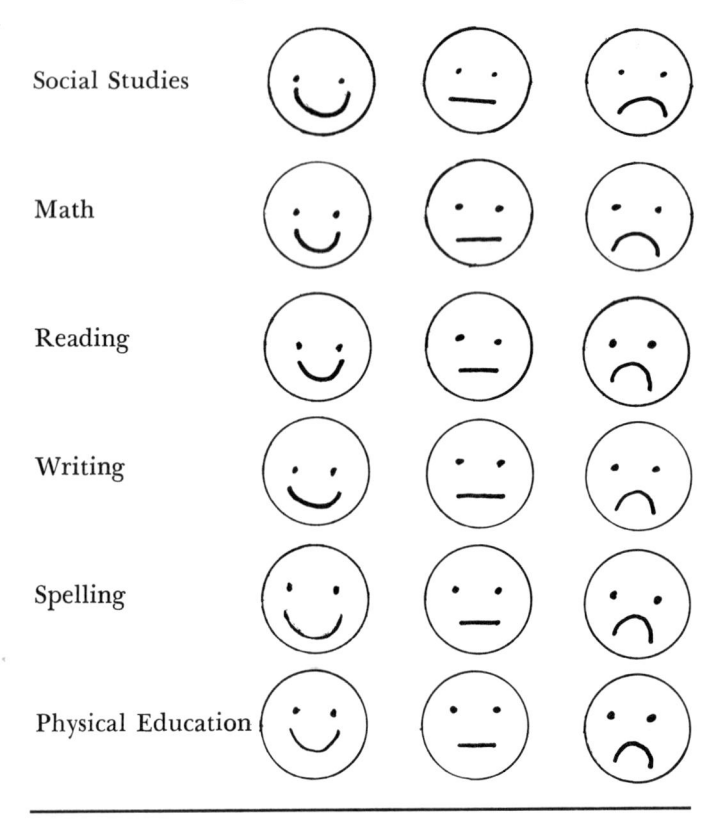

Social Studies	☺	😐	☹
Math	☺	😐	☹
Reading	☺	😐	☹
Writing	☺	😐	☹
Spelling	☺	😐	☹
Physical Education	☺	😐	☹

Figure 391

    Use older students to administer the questionnaire to small groups of children.

3. After the data are collected, involve the students in summing the responses for each category and making statements about the results (that is, in making inferences).

4. Allow the questionnaires to be answered anonymously, but also consider adding a Boy _____

Girl _____ checkoff category and summarizing the data accordingly.
5. Collect data from other classrooms of the same and different levels and involve the students in making comparative statements.

392 *Instructional Attitude Study*

Use the same questionnaire format described in Activity 391 but concentrate on teaching activities/strategies rather than subject areas. The list in Figure 392 (p. 244) might be useful as you make selections for your particular situation.

393 *Alternative Schools*

Allow students to learn about alternatives to their own schools. Most students are in schools that are traditional in terms of the physical facilities, course scheduling, and course offerings. However, alternatives exist in the form of open-space architecture (physical facilities) and of varied curricular offerings and scheduling such as may be found in open and free schools. If such alternatives are in your district, your students can then visit the facilities and make comparisons with their own set up.

Similarly, invitations could be extended to alternative school students to visit your facilities and serve as resource persons. If your district has no alternative schools, then establish contact with school districts such as St. Paul Unified or Minneapolis Unified School Districts and seek informational brochures on the alternatives they provide.

Focus questions

What do you like most about the alternative school?
What do you like least?
How is the alternative school like ours?
How is it different?

How I Usually Feel About Doing Certain Things During Social Studies

Activity	😊	😐	☹
Listening to the teacher			
Listening to others			
Looking at a film			
Reading in books			
Making things			
Painting, coloring			
Answering questions in the book			
Discussing questions in class			
Working on class projects			
Writing reports			

Figure 392

394 *Arranging School Space*

Using various size boxes and containers (such as shoe boxes and milk cartons) to represent various structures, involve the students in laying out their idea for the best arrangement of school facilities. By selecting from various size boxes, the students can decide the relative sizes of the various modules (such as kindergarten, sixth-grade classroom, the principal's office). (See Figure 394.)

Students should justify why they located structures where they do (Why is the kindergarten near the cafeteria but away from the sixth grade classroom? Why is the teacher's workroom in the center of 'your' school?) Students could work in small groups of two or three persons and various plans could be compared as well as individ-

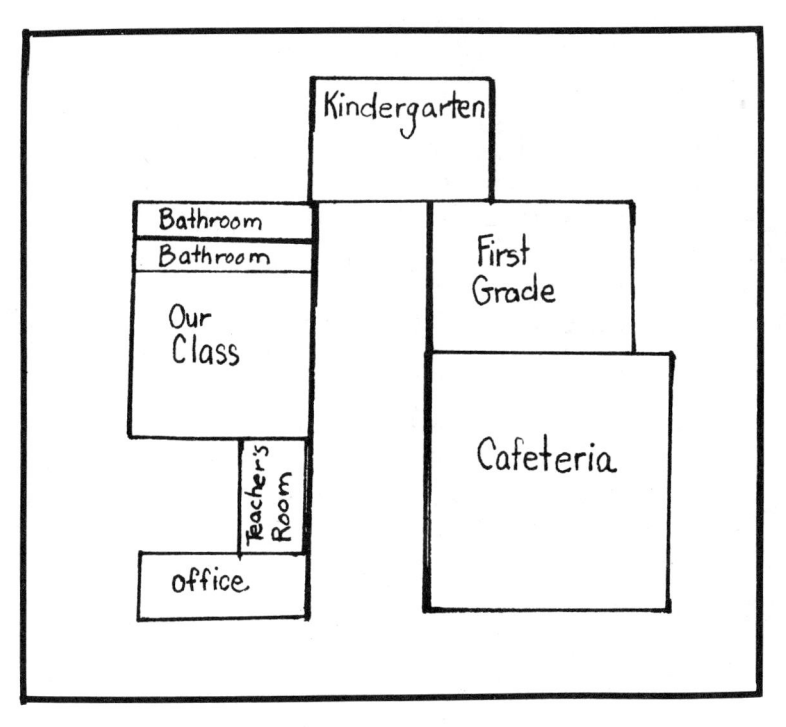

Figure 394

ually defended. 'Ideal schools' should be compared with the school the students are currently attending.

395 *Using Classroom Space*

Have the students make guesses concerning why the furniture and materials in the classroom are arranged as they are. Invite the students to offer suggestions for rearranging the room or a section of it. Any suggestions should be backed up with statements concerning how the classroom would thereby be improved. Even consider pushing everything toward one corner of the room and allowing the class, or a subgroup of students, to rearrange the environment. A main purpose of the activity is to help the students perceive a relationship between function and the use of space.

396 *Learning Situations*

Ask students to bring pictures to school that show someone learning. As pictures are brought in, have each student identify what is being learned, who the teacher is, and who the learner is. Encourage the sharing of personal photographs that depict the child's early learnings.

Consider starting a collage that requires students to group the pictures into school learnings and out-of-school learnings. Have the students use the collage display to make statements about varied kinds of learning situations and where they usually take place. More mature students could also discuss why schools seem to be the most used place for certain learnings to take place.

397 *School Rules*

Have students brainstorm all the school rules they can think of for each of the following activities:

When and where running can take place
When and where eating can take place
When and where play can take place
When and where talking can take place
When and where they can walk
When they can leave the classroom
When they must be in the classroom

Follow-up questions

How did you learn these rules? (This will require some probing. Children will sometimes answer that they have always known the rules or that they 'just know' what they are.)

What happens to the person who does not follow the rules?

How is it decided what is to happen to a rule breaker?

How are rules changed at school?

Who is responsible for enforcing the rules? Why?

398 *Rules From the Past*

Have the students discuss with parents and/or grandparents the rules that were in effect during their school days.

Focus questions

What was the punishment when a rule was broken?

What are some rules you had in your school that we do not have now?

Why do you think that school is (more, less) strict today?

Do you think this is OK? Why?

Follow-up

Have the students share the results of their discussions, comparing the rules and punishment procedures in their school with those experienced by their parents and/or grandparents.

☼ 399 *Changing School Rules*

Have the students react in written form to the following questions:

1. What rule at school would you most like to see changed?
2. Describe the changes you want.
3. Why is your suggestion for a change a good one?
4. How might you go about getting the rule changed? (Who would have to be on your side? How would you go about getting them on your side?)

The follow-up activity might take the form of a class commitment to work toward changing a specific rule or encouraging and supporting individuals to seek rule changes.

Variation

Use the same procedures to discuss and act on *changes* they think are necessary in their school.

☼ 400 *"Why Do We Have Schools?" Survey*

Distribute a questionnaire with one open-ended question:
   We have schools in order to help kids _____
_____.

Students write out the rest of the sentence and add any other statements they wish. Involve the students in classifying the responses and in making a statement about the results.

Follow-up questions

1. Where else, besides school, do these learnings take place?
2. Who else besides the teachers at school help us with these learnings?
3. Considering our answers to questions (1) and (2), are schools really necessary? Why?

401 *Using the School Survey Data*

Hint 1

Younger students can take turns recording (versus writing out) their responses to the sentence stimulus in Activity 400. An older student or paraprofessional can be in charge of tape recording each student's response. (Note: Do not record the sentence stimulus for each student; just the responses.) Afterwards, play the tape for the students, asking them to listen for "what students say most often." In addition, consider using variations of the older questions already suggested.

Hint 2

Involve the class in making predictions on how students at other grade levels will respond to the sentence stimulus. Then have them collect the relevant data, using tape recorders, a check list, or letting the respondents write out their answers.

402 *School Attitudinal Survey*

Distribute a simple attitudinal inventory like the one shown in Figure 402, p. 250.

Count the number of responses for each face and

250   SECTION 3

Mark an X through the face that best shows how you usually feel about school.

☺ 😐 ☹

Check what you are: Boy _____   Girl _____

Figure 402

have the students use the resultant data to describe how children in their class feel about school.

Follow-up possibilities

Repeat this experiment with other groups and compare to previous findings. Students/researchers might work in pairs—one reading the question and the other recording the responses. Such research pairs can include students from different age levels (for example, a five-year-old could work with an eleven-year-old).

※ 403 *Inventory of Schools*

Bring in multiple copies of your city's telephone Yellow Pages as well as the classified sections of the local newspapers. Involve the students in using these data sources to list the different kinds of schools (such as barber college, flying school, dance schools) in their community.

※ 404 *Job-Oriented Schools*

Invite a teacher in from a job-oriented school (such as a beauty college or a business school) to discuss the school in such terms as: its purposes, what the students are like, what happens in the courses, and where some of the graduates are now working.

✤ 405 *Teacher Interviews*

Invite teachers within your school to the classroom to be interviewed concerning their feelings about their job. A questioning guide like the one shown in Figure 405 might be created by the students before the interview is to occur.

Teacher Questioning Guide
1. How did you decide to become a teacher?
2. What are some of the things that are important for being a good teacher?
3. What do you especially like about being a teacher?
4. What are some of the things you must do as a teacher that you do not enjoy?

Figure 405

Hint

If several teachers are to be interviewed, involve the class in a summary statement concerning how each teacher responded to each of the main questions. You will then have a data base for comparing responses among the teachers.

✤ 406 *School Problems Survey*

Students can interview various school personnel (such as the principal, teachers, custodians, road crossing guards, etc.) to determine what each thinks is the biggest problem faced each day in the job. Students can then compile a list of problems and decide how they might help someone with a problem. For example, a road crossing guard might have trouble keeping younger children together while they cross the street. Older student volunteers might be organized to offer assistance.

407 *School Time Capsule*

Involve the students in deciding what should be placed in a time capsule to help people understand one hundred years from now what school was like. The time capsule can be simulated by using any container such as a shoe box, produce box, or gallon ice cream container, and having students actually place the objects in the container.

Follow-up suggestion

Give the time capsule, with its contents, to another group of students and ask them to draw inferences about school that are represented. Compare these inferences with those intended by the students who selected the artifacts for that time capsule.

408 *Games Survey*

Display and discuss such games as Flinch, Sorry, Yahtzee, Aggravation, Monopoly, checkers, and chess. Also, talk about various card games (such as Fish, Old Maid, Hearts). Poll the class on which of the games they know how to play. Call in various individuals to indicate when they learned the game, who taught them the game, and how they were taught.

409 *Students as Teachers*

Place students in the teaching role by having them teach someone else how to play a game such as Yahtzee. Depending on the maturity of the 'teachers,' ask them to respond to the following questions:

1. What did you do to teach the other person how to play the game?
   Read the instructions to the other person

Played the game with the other person
Asked questions
2. What problems did you have? How did you take care of those problems?
3. Did the other person learn from what you did? How do you know?

Suggestions:

1. Involve three persons in each learning group: one person as a teacher, another as the learner, and a nonparticipating person as an observer collecting data around the preceding three questions.
2. Consider the possibility of mixing roles (teacher, learner, observer) among varied grade levels.
3. Consider sharing your own experiences regarding problems you encounter while teaching a concept, procedure, skill, etc.

410 *Student-Teacher Attitudes*

After a teaching/learning experience like the one described in Activity 409, have 'teachers' as well as the learners fill out a brief attitudinal inventory like the one in Figure 410.

How I Felt:

At the beginning

While the (game) was
 being explained

At the end

Figure 410

Ask individual volunteers to explain why they marked their attitudinal inventory as they did. Consider sharing relevant experiences and feelings you have had both as a teacher and as a learner.

411 *Writing School History*

Involve students in developing the history of their school. This history could be very brief and only include one or two focal questions from this list of possibilities:

- When was the school originally built?
- What was the neighborhood like at the time the school was first built?
- How has the school (physical structure) changed over the years?
- When did classes first begin in this school?
- Has our classroom always been used for children of our age level?
- Who were some of the first teachers at this school? Where are they now? What do they remember about this school?
- Who were some of the first graduates of our school? What are they doing now? What do they remember about the school? How do they feel about schools today? In what ways is our school different from the way it was when they were students? What is the same?
- Where are the school's former principals? What can they tell us about the school's development?

TOPIC: NEWS/NEWSPAPERS

Activities

✺ **412** *Locating News Sections*

Help students become acquainted with the various sections of the newspaper by having them locate any information on the following topics:

   The President of the United States
   Other national and international news
   Sports
   Weather
   Movies
   Comics
   Letters to the editor
   Political cartoons
   Community news
   Stock market

Alternative procedure

Have the students suggest sections or categories of news found in the paper.

✺ **413** *Comparing Newspapers*

Obtain multiple copies of different newspapers available in your community. Students can compare the newspapers according to such characteristics as:

   Frequency of publication
   Number of pages
   Number of sections
   Price
   Circulation
   Absence or presence of particular comic strips

Possible focus questions

1. True or False: The bigger the newspaper is (number of pages), the more it costs. Give evidence for your answer.
2. True or False: Bigger newspapers have more pages of advertising, but they do not really have more news. Give evidence.
3. True or False: All newspapers contain the same kind of weather information. Offer evidence.

414 *Comparing Reports*

This activity is to help students understand that different kinds of newspapers include different kinds of information.

Make available multiple copies of two or three different newspapers with varying circulations (such as neighborhood; suburban newspapers, as well as those serving a broader audience such as the Los Angeles *Times* and the New York *Times*). Using the newspapers, the students can work together to respond to the following kinds of focus questions:

1. Which newspaper is better for finding out what the temperature yesterday was for _____ (the community in which the school is located)?
2. Which newspaper is more likely to have news about some event at our school? Why?
3. Which newspaper would be better if you were looking for a job? Why?
4. Which newspaper is the better one for finding out about professional _____ (football, basketball, baseball, etc. that is, whatever the season is when you conduct this lesson)? Why?
5. Find a story that is reported in each newspaper. How is the reporting the same? How is it different?

415　*The Daily Changes*

Accumulate multiple copies of one newspaper for one week. Involve the students in such questions as the following:

1. Not including Sunday's paper, which day's paper was the largest? the smallest?
2. What connection, if any, do you think there might be between a day of the week and having a large paper, and another day of the week and having a paper with fewer pages?
3. What sections of the newspaper are found in the paper each day? What sections are found only on certain days? Why do you think some sections are included everyday and others aren't?
4. Name some companies, products, services or others that advertise in the newspaper everyday. Notice whether or not their ads were usually in about the same section of the newspaper from day to day.

Suggestion

In working with Question 2 above, consider involving the students in collecting and processing data. A graph like the one shown in Figure 415 could be useful.

Day of the week	Total number of newspaper pages. □ = 5 pages
_____	
_____	
_____	
_____	
_____	

Figure 415

416 Ad Placement

Use a chart like the one shown in Figure 416 to involve students in hypothesizing on the best location in a newspaper for various kinds of ads.

Follow-up possibilities

1. Ask individual students to state their choices and give reasons.
2. On a master chart, tally the various student re-

Directions: For each ad mark an X in the box that shows your choice for the best section to run the ad.

Section

Advertising	Front	Sports	Local news	Movies, theater	Business	Editorials
Supermarket food specials						
Auto tires						
Refrigerators and other appliances						
Men's clothing						
Women's shoes						
Banks, savings & loans						
Toys						

Figure 416

sponses. Have students make statements regarding the processed data.
3. Have students go through newspapers and determine where the different kinds of advertising are actually located.
4. Compare Number 3 with Number 2.

417 *News-Ad Patterns*

Cut out four or five strips of butcher paper (each approximately 3′ ×5′). Label each strip according to a different section of the newspaper as shown in Figure 417, and display in the classroom.

Involve groups of students in cutting out all advertising for a particular section and pasting it on the appropriate sheet of butcher paper. Students can then scan the 'data' and make statements about any patterns they can detect.

Note

This activity could serve nicely as a follow-up to Activity 416.

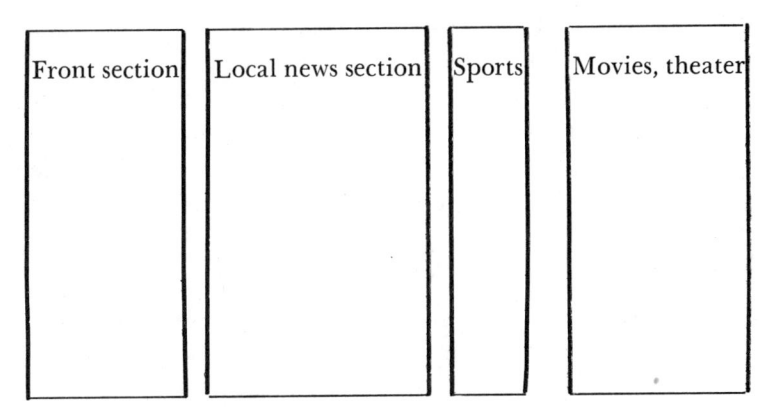

Front section	Local news section	Sports	Movies, theater

Figure 417

418 Locating Information

Distribute newspapers to individual students or groups of students. Ask them to locate information like that shown in the worksheet in Figure 418.

Information Worksheet

1. What is playing tonight at the _____ theater? (Name a specific theater in your community.) _____

2. Name several places in the world where it rained yesterday. _____, _____, _____

3. Where was the President of the United States yesterday? _____

4. Who won the game between _____ and _____ yesterday? _____

Figure 418

This activity could be turned into a game in which groups of students race to give a correct response.

419 Newscast Analysis

Tape record a TV or radio newscast. After playing only one minute of the recording, ask the class to name and describe the news stories they heard. List these stories on the board. Repeat the procedure for four or five additional segments of one minute each. Have the students look at the listings and elaborate on the reported news.

Possible follow-up questions

1. How many different news stories were reported during the first minute?
2. Why do you think the news editor decided to have these stories reported first?
3. How are the stories from the first minute of the

newscast like those from the other minutes? How are they different?

✵ 420   *Comparing News Reports*

Follow-up activity to Activity 419

Have students examine a newspaper published on the same day as the recorded newscast and compare the two news sources.

Possible organizing questions for this activity:

1. In what ways is the front section of the newspaper like the first five minutes of the newscast? How is it different?
2. How would you answer someone who said that a person learns more news by reading a newspaper than by listening to (and looking at) a newscast? Give reasons for what you say. (Try to have the students refer to specific parts/stories of the newspaper and newscast when they give their answers.)

✵ 421   *Span of Influence*

Involve the students in generating a list of all the newspapers that are home delivered in their community. Using wall-sized maps, pinpoint your community and extend a piece of yarn out to the origin of each newspaper on the list.

Possible focus questions

1. Which home delivered newspaper comes from the farthest distance?
2. Why do you think that some people buy this paper rather than, or in addition to, those that are published nearer to where they live?

422 Newsstand Analysis

Have students guess which cities in the world have newspapers that can be purchased at a newsstand in their own community. Record the predictions as well as some of the reasons. Visit a large news shop and list the titles, or buy copies, of the out-of-town and out-of-state publications. Compare what is available to the previous predictions.

Follow-up

Have the students mark the location on a wall map of each city represented by the various newspapers and use yarn to connect that location with the location of their city.

Ask: Why are newspapers from distant locations sold in our city?

423 Comparing Daily Editions

Collect and distribute different editions of the *same* newspaper. How are the front pages alike? How different? What reasons might the publisher have for changing the various editions?

424 News Emphasis Reporting

Select a current, specific news topic to serve as a *News Emphasis*. Over a period of several days (determined by how newsworthy the emphasis is) have students collect and report daily on the emphasis news, excluding all other news topics. Such a procedure can be geared to varied age groups through the particular news emphasis selected. An advantage of emphasis news is that students are provided an opportunity to relate news reports meaningfully over a period of days, as well as to have a specific focus for making news selections. Perhaps the students can become involved in determining what the news emphasis should be.

425 'Selling' the Newsworthy

In deciding on a news emphasis (see Activity 424) or in summarizing the highlights of several days of news, consider having students 'sell' to others what was most newsworthy. A group of five or so students might be designated as prospective 'buyers' who will listen to each sales presentation and then make a decision.

426 Controversial Involvement

Introduce a news item that is controversial and display that item. Several days later call on each student to take a position regarding the controversy.

427 Newspaper Jobs

Generate a list of all jobs involved in getting a newspaper to the doorstep or to the newsstand. Depending on the maturity of the students, have them sequence the jobs from the beginning of production to delivery.

428 The Newsmaker Game

Introduce the *Newsmaker Game*. Review with the students the names of newsmakers for the week and write the names of each person on an index card. Individuals from teams of students draw a card and make a statement about the person listed. A group of two to four students can serve as judges of the accuracy of each statement. Each accurate statement is worth one point for the team.

429 Newsmaker Review

This is a variation of Activity 428.
   Save the newsmaker cards for each week and use as bonus cards. Students who make a correct statement on a

newsmaker from the current week are then allowed to select a bonus card. A correct response is equal to the number of weeks ago a name appeared. Thus, a name that appeared in the news four weeks ago is worth four points for a valid statement about the person's newsworthy contribution.

430 *Newsmaker Password*

Use the newsmaker cards described in Activities 428 and 429 in the context of playing a game similar to Password.

Individual members from team A and team B sit across the table from their team partners. A newsmaker card is drawn and a member of team A offers a one-word clue to help the partner guess the name on the card. If the correct answer is given, team A receives 15 points. A new card is then drawn and the next round initiated by the team B representatives. If the response is incorrect, then 14 points (vs. 15) would now be available as a member of team B provides a clue for the partner. Each time an incorrect response is given, the name on the card is worth one less point.

Guessing four names correctly is usually sufficient for one game play. The clues are ordinarily single words and may be proper names. Communication through charades is not allowed.

431 *Tag-Board News*

Upper-grade students can not only list the newsmakers for a week but also compose one-sentence statements describing what the newsmaker did.

Write a statement or two for each newsmaker on tag-board strips. After a name is drawn, the student can go through the tag-board strips and locate and read one statement that is appropriate. The activity can be turned into a game by choosing teams and assigning points for correct responses.

✺ 432 *News Vocabulary Logs*

Record the key vocabulary words that come up during each day of student news reporting. Enter each word on an index card or on a strip of tag-board. Students can select a word card and then retrieve a news article from the news bulletin board that is relevant to that word. The student then uses the word in a sentence that reflects the selected news item.

✺ 433 *News Twenty Questions*

From appropriate stacks of cards, a news statement, or the name of a newsmaker, or a vocabulary word that came up during news reporting is drawn by a team member. (Refer to the previous activities for ideas on generating these cards.) Other team members are then allowed to ask twenty questions in order to guess correctly what was drawn. The person who draws the card can only respond with *yes* or *no* answers.

✺ 434 *Editorial Stands*

Select a controversial news item and have different students take different sides of the issue by writing an editorial for their positions.

✺ 435 *News Rewrites*

Sometimes it is possible to generate information surrounding a controversy. For example, possibly within the community controversy arises concerning whether an older group of homes should be removed and replaced with a shopping center. An open city council meeting is held to discuss the matter. Have students rewrite newspaper accounts of the meeting to reflect specific, but varying, positions.

436 *Birthdate News*

Sometimes parents save newspapers that were published on the dates their children were born. Ask students to check with their parents and report back on what was happening on their birthdate, what TV programs were listed for that day, what was happening in the sports world, what movies were playing, how much such items as a stereo or a refrigerator cost, who was president of the United States, etc. Ask each presenter to make comparisons with the present.

TOPICS OF STUDY   267

TOPIC: HUMAN EQUALITY

Activities

☼ 437   Ad Analysis

Cut out all advertisements from available magazines and newspapers and separate out all ads containing pictures of people. These 'person ads' are then further divided into three groups: females only; males only; both males and females. The students can look for relationships between the persons shown and what products or services are being advertised. (See Figures 437a, below, and 437b, p. 268.)

Figure 437a. (Reprinted by permission of Olken's, Inc., Wellesley, Mass.)

268   SECTION 3

Figure 437b.   (Reprinted by permission of Olken's, Inc., Wellesley, Mass.)

438 Selling with Physical Characteristics

This activity can be a follow-up to Activity 437.

Students are asked to find advertising that includes an attractive person who apparently has little or nothing to do with the product or service being advertised. For example, a woman in a bikini might be selling auto tires or holding out the keys for a car rental. The Yellow Pages are an excellent source for this activity. Look under such classification as: Answering Bureaus, Car Rentals, and Eye Glasses.

Similarly, students can find examples of athletes endorsing such items and services as deodorants, beer, tires, hair spray, and car rental agencies.

Discuss the connection, if any, between the expertise of the person(s) shown and the products or services being advertised.

439 Male/Female Job Survey

Students can look through their reading and social studies books and identify the jobs shown for males and females. An observation guide like the one in Figure 439, p. 270, might be used.

Older students can read for such information as well as use the pictures.

Possible follow-up questions

1. Describe the kinds of jobs shown for (a) males, (b) females, (e.g., inside, outside, working with their hands, 'heavy' work, housework, 'out of the house,' etc.).
2. Can (could, should) men do the jobs shown for the women? Why?

Observation Guide

Book _____ My name _____

Page   Job that is shown   Who is shown doing the job

Figure 439

3. Can (could, should) women do the jobs shown for the men? Why?

440   *Role Analysis*

In Activity 439, *jobs* was used as the key category for a content analysis of male or female participation. Other categories for extending this activity include:

Roles in family life (e.g., who is feeding the baby? washing the car? hammering and sawing?)
Playing games (e.g., who is playing quiet games? competitive games?)
Behavior (e.g., who is happy? sad? crying? fighting? arguing? receiving praise?)

Focus question

Even though our books (advertisements, etc.) show _____ (name a specific behavior), is it possible for _____ (males, females) to also do this? Why?

TOPICS OF STUDY 271

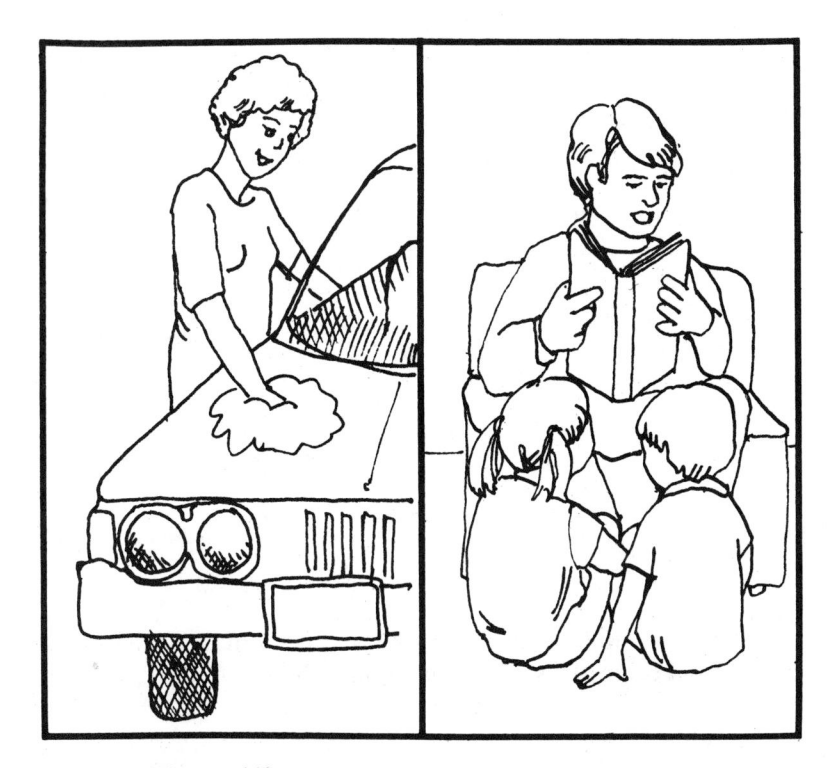

Figure 440

441 Male/Female Teacher Survey

Have students tally the distribution of male/female teachers in their school. A chart like the one in Figure 441, p. 272, might be useful.

Possible follow-up questions

1. Look at the tallies that have been made and offer a sentence that describes what you observe.
2. In your opinion, should there be more male teachers at the lower grade levels? Why? Why do you think there are not more in our school? Are other schools like us? How could we find out?

Grade Level	Teacher's Name	Man	Woman
Kindergarten	Miss Jones		x
	Mrs. Perkins		x
	Miss Johnson		x
1st Grade	_____		
	_____		
	_____		
2nd Grade	_____		
	_____		
	_____		

Figure 441

3. In your opinion, should there be more female (male) teachers in the sixth grade at our school? Why? Why do you think there are not more in our school? Are other schools like us? How could we find out?

442 *Male/Female Distribution— Nonteaching Jobs*

Use Activity 439 to analyze the male/female distribution for other school-related jobs such as: principal(s), custodians, cafeteria workers, secretaries, road crossing guards, bus drivers, nurses.

443 *Changes in Hiring Practices*

Invite representatives from such organizations as the police department, fire department, or telephone company to visit the classroom and discuss how male/female job roles have changed over the past few years.

444 *Physicians—Male/Female*

Using the telephone Yellow Pages, students can tally the number of male and female physicians in their community. Older students could convert the tally sums into percentages.

Focal questions

1. What do our data show?
2. Why do you think there are more men than women doctors?

445 *Commercial Artists, Accountants, etc.*

Besides *physicians* (see Activity 444), consider using additional categories including: commercial artists, accountants, dentists, attorneys, optometrists, chiropractors, architects, photographers, veterinarians, insurance agents.

446 *Daily Observations*

Ask the students to observe in their daily lives when a role is taken that is different from what some people might think is the usual way. (See Figure 446, p. 274.)

Examples

The telephone information operator is a man
The telephone repair person is a woman
A male nurse
A female physician
A father feeding a baby, changing a diaper, preparing a meal, vacuuming
A woman bus driver
A female letter carrier
A woman newscaster
A woman qualifier for the Indianapolis 500 race

Figure 446

Provide a period of time each day for a week for the reporting of any observations.

Possible focus questions

1. Why did we have some disagreement over whether or not several of the things reported were unusual?
2. Why is it that we do not expect the telephone operator to be a man? etc.

447 *Sex-Role Scenarios*

Students can create and then write or tell stories around such 'possible' titles as:

Mary Adams—Our 42nd President of the United States.

Glenda Jones—The new shortstop for the Los Angeles Dodgers.

Michelle Smith—Discoverer of a new chemical for controlling cancer.

448 *Pronouns*

Have students look through the reading material in the classroom (reading and social studies textbooks, library books, etc.) for evidence of using pronouns of specific genders when describing personal behavior, roles, positions, etc.

Examples

Referring to a principal as *he,* but a teacher as *she.*

Question	Boys	Girls	No Difference
Who has more trouble in school?			
Who behaves better in school?			
Who is smarter?			
Who is more neat?			
Who are the better readers?			
Who is better at sports?			

Figure 449

449 *Boy/Girl Survey*

Duplicate and distribute multiple copies of a questionnaire like the one in Figure 449. Each student can go to another class and tally the reactions of several individuals.

Total and display the results. Allow the students to summarize and discuss differences of opinion as well as to offer reasons concerning why people probably voted the way they did.

Suggestion

Interview both lower and upper grade students and compare for any response differences.

TOPIC: ENVIRONMENTAL EDUCATION

Activities

☼ 450 *Water Conservation Study*

Run a class study on the effects of publicizing and implementing various water conservation procedures. First, generate a list of ways to cut down on water consumption.

Examples

> Do not use the toilet as a trash can; cut down on length of showers
> Do not leave the water running while toothbrushing or shaving
> Run dishwashers and clothes washers only when filled
> Store a jug of ice water in the refrigerator rather than run water for a while in order to get a cold drink

Next, help each student learn how to read a water meter. *Note:* Check with your local water district office for a supply of booklets on water conservation, including how to read a meter.

Now, have the students record the water meter reading for their homes on the same day and repeat a week later. Then, begin a home water savings program that includes implementing the previously listed water conservation measures. Record the water meter reading one week later. A student worksheet like the one in Figure 450 can be useful.

Now involve the class in sharing individual results and compiling class totals. Have the students use the compiled data to make statements (inferences) regarding the effects of the one-week conservation program.

☼ 451 *Watering the Garden*

Locate the school's water meter. Have the custodian turn on the water sprinkler and observe the meter dial move

278   SECTION 3

Water Meter Worksheet

NAME _____
Before home water savings program:
1st water meter reading _____   Date _____
2nd water meter reading _____   Date _____
Difference between 1st and 2nd readings _____ = A
After home water savings program:
Start (Enter the 2nd
  reading from above _____   Date _____
End (Reading one week
  after the 2nd reading _____   Date _____
Difference between the
  starting and ending readings _____ = B
Difference between
  A and B = _____.

Figure 450

for precisely one minute. Multiply the number of gallons used in one minute by sixty for the quantity used per hour. Ask the custodian or gardener to estimate how long the sprinkler is ordinarily left running. Estimate the hundreds of gallons used weekly to water the school's lawns and gardens.

452   *House Design of the Future*

Involve students in drawing plans, or constructing a model, to represent a house of the future. First, discuss and research how such topics as the following might be considered in planning future homes:

New forms of heating and cooling
Trash removal
Low maintenance exteriors and interiors that seldom, if ever, need painting or replacing

Low maintenance as well as smaller garden areas
Noise insulation

✺ 453 Planning Tomorrow's Community

Especially if an activity like Activity 452 goes successfully, consider having the students design a community for the future. Blocks of wood, shoe cartons, and butcher paper would be useful in such a project. If petty cash is available, consider purchasing various size strips of balsa wood at a toy or hobby store and use for model construction.

Consider such topics as the following for possible implications for future community planning

> Traffic systems (monorail? people movers? automobile ban in certain sectors of the community?)
> Trash disposal via chutes and mechanized conveyors (versus trash cans and trucks) with automated selection and sorting of materials for recycling
> Desalinization and use of sea water
> Increased use of nonsoil procedures for crop production
> Changes in car design and usage (e.g., fenders that 'give' and bounce back on impact; failsafe passenger protection systems; reductions in the noise of automobile starting, acceleration, etc.; the use of alternative fuels such as electricity, diesel, methane, and propane; automated parking lots)
> Increased cultivation of food crops from the ocean

✺ 454 Noise Pollution Survey

Students can survey the school environment and list the various sources and examples of noise pollution.

Examples

> Public address systems
> Lawn mowers and school buses that operate during class time

People talking outside of classrooms
Playground activity
People carrying on extended conversations in the library
Cafeteria noises
Workmen carrying on nonwork conversations
School bells rung to summon the custodian or principal
Classroom intercoms used during class time

Involve the class in thinking of possible ways of bringing about changes and in selecting the best solutions for actual implementation.

455 *Electrical Use Survey*

Students can survey the use of electricity in their homes and their reliance on it by using an observation form like the one in Figure 455.

456 *Values Survey*

Sometimes we behave as though electrical energy 'costs,' but human energy is 'free.' Thus, hanging clothes in the basement during the winter is not always a viable alternative to an automatic dryer. This activity can help students reflect on their values regarding conservation.

Direct the students to consider each item entered on their home observation sheet (see Figure 455) and check as follows: "Mark an *OK* if you feel you could get along without it, write an *O* of it does not matter whether or not you have it, and write a *NO* if you would not be willing to give up the item." Have the students think of, or write out, a sentence that summarizes their feelings about how far they could go without the use of electricity as reflected in their responses. Allow volunteers to share their statements.

Observation Sheet—Things That Use Electricity in the Home	
Name: _____	
Runs on Electricity	How the Same Work Might be Done Without the Use of Electricity—Including Batteries
Dishwasher	Wash dishes by hand
Hairdryer	Use a towel; the sun
TV	Nothing else to use
Lights	Candles, fire, matches
Clotheswasher	Wash by hand

Figure 455

☼ 457 *Electrical Awareness Morning*

Have an 'electrical awareness' morning (or hour) at school. With advance warning, turn off the school's electricity for one hour and have the students note everything that stops running as well as the changes people make in order to maintain a normal schedule.

☼ 458 *Invention and Energy Conservation*

Involve students in locating instances in which energy (human resources as well as natural resources) is being saved

Change, Discovery, Invention	Possible Effects On Energy Consumption (Human and Natural Resources Included)
Drip-dry clothing	Less time in ironing
Permanent-press clothing	Washing at home instead of use of dry cleaners
Radial tires	Replacement less often than other types
New car oil changes at 6,000 instead of 3,000 miles	Oil savings
Increased gas mileage for some new cars	Gasoline savings

Figure 458

as the result of changes, discoveries, and inventions. Advertising and adults can serve as sources of relevant information. A chart like the one in Figure 458 might be used to organize the information.

459 *Future Inventions*

Have the students think of additional improvements in clothing, cars, TVs, use of 'other' natural resources, etc., that could lead to increased energy conservation.

Examples

Clothing materials that are soil-resistant

Modular car parts that the owner can easily replace—including engine parts

More effective ways of collecting water runoff and transporting it to more arid locales

Harnessing energy from the action of ocean waves

Extended and improved uses of solar energy
Harvesting the ocean for our food supply.

☼ 460 *Environmental Impact Study*

Involve the students in an 'environmental impact study' of changes (or lack of changes) in the use of the neighborhood environment.

For example, the study might be focused on a new structure being erected on a previously empty lot, or the tearing down of an existing one-story structure for replacement with a multilevel building, or the tearing down of an old building, long deserted and frequently vandalized. Topics of the study could include the land use consequences on the local environment in terms of: automobile traffic, noise levels, increased numbers of people, and visual pollution.

Section 4

AFFECTIVE / EVALUATIVE DOMAIN

RATIONALE

Basically, three main categories of objectives prevail in social studies education: understandings (e.g., concepts, topics of study), skills (e.g., maps, globes, research, listening, etc.), and the affective. Many books and articles have been written on values clarification, moral education, and confluent education and reflect several affective possibilities that might be pursued in classrooms. Similarly, formal procedures and materials for evaluating student progress toward instructional objectives are plentiful.

However, the purpose of this section is to give indications of how a focus on the learner's self-esteem and self-awareness can be used in the pursuit of both affective instructional objectives and certain evaluative purposes. For example, several of the evaluative activities described require student reaction to, and awareness of, the instructional procedures and materials used. The data collected from these activities can be used by the teacher to plan future instructional procedures and can serve as a supplement to more traditional approaches for assessing student progress toward specific instructional objectives.

AFFECTIVE/EVALUATIVE ACTIVITIES

☼ 461 *Collecting Attitudinal Data on the Controversial*

After discussion of a controversial topic or event, distribute a handout containing a rectangle divided into tenths. See Figure 461.

Ask the students to indicate by filling in the boxes how strongly they feel toward a particular position. If they feel *very strongly* toward the position, then they would fill in all ten boxes. Filling in no boxes would indicate a very passive attitude. Allow volunteers to discuss their responses.

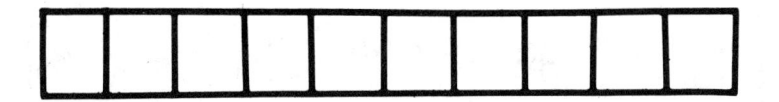

Figure 461

☼ 462 *Positive Characteristics*

Involve the class in listing a series of descriptive words or phrases that other people might like to hear about themselves.

Examples

Nice looking
Nice dresser
Fun to be around
Good worker
Cheerful
Good student
Fast runner
Funny
Strong

288   SECTION 4

> Todd H.
> fast runner
> very friendly
> nice smile
> fun to play with
> good at adding

Figure 462

Involve the class in making selections from the list or in creating new words or phrases for each member of the class. Write the results on index cards and display in the classroom. See Figure 462.

463 Celebrity of the Week

Have a *Classroom Celebrity of the Week*. Have the remaining students anonymously enter on 4″ × 6″ index cards at least one positive thing about the celebrity and deposit the cards in a ballot-type box (e.g., an old shoe box with a slit in the cover). See Figure 463, p. 289.

Note

Consider screening the cards for negative comments before giving them to the student.

AFFECTIVE/EVALUATIVE 289

Figure 463

✣ 464 *Ads for Friends*

Have the students create ads or posters that publicize the best characteristics of a friend.

✣ 465 *Mood Charts*

Create a *Mood Chart*.

Display a list of names of everyone in the room. Using three different colors, cut out squares (1″ × 1″) of construction paper, so that one set of three squares is available per student. Each color is to reflect a mood, such as black equals gloomy, green equals OK, yellow equals really good. Each morning, students pin one of the colored squares opposite their name. (Suggestion: include yourself!) Discussion might follow on how those students who are gloomy might be helped through the day as well. Also share the reasons that some students are really feeling good. Do not force anyone to share his or her feelings or even to participate in the activity.

466 *Autobiographical Displays*

Provide each student with bulletin board space and a display table for one week in order to create an *Autobiographical Display*. The display might include snapshots, trophies, ribbons, prized work, artifacts, and any other memorabilia the student cares to share. Have the student present the display to the class.

Follow-up possibility

Have the students refer to the display and write a letter to the autobiographical author that includes at least one positive statement concerning the display as well as the person responsible for the display.

467 *Proud Tables*

In one corner of the room, designate a *Proud Table*. Once a week, let students place something on the table that gives them particular pride (such as something they have made, a school paper, a note from their parents thanking them for something they did, a note they have written concerning a personal accomplishment or service performed). Give each contributor the opportunity to share this proud activity.

Suggestion

Keep a record of the students who contribute. Offer assistance to students who seem to have difficulty in thinking of something of which to be personally proud.

468   Adopt A Senior Citizen

As a class, 'adopt' an elderly person who is confined to his or her place of residence. Exchange weekly letters, and when possible, telephone or visit the person.

469   I Would Like To Thank You . . .

Have the students select a well-known person and write or dictate a letter of appreciation. The letter could be as simple as completing the sentence, "I would like to thank you for . . ." The idea is especially useful as part of the observance of holidays.

470   Enjoyment Display

Each student brings in one object such as a shoe box or a bottle. Using old magazines, newspapers, and catalogs, or drawing original art, the students decorate their object with pictures of things they enjoy.

Follow-up

Each student displays and shares his or her work.

Alternative

Objects are exchanged and interpreted by someone other than the owner.

471   Conversation Prediction

Display a picture that contains two or more persons who contrast sharply in their appearance. For example, the picture might show a middle-aged person in business suit, with attaché case in hand, talking to a college-age student

292   SECTION 4

Figure 471

with long hair and beard, dressed in jeans, T-shirt, and sandals, as in Figure 471. Tell the class that the two people are discussing the proper dress when dining out. Have the class create dialogue that might be going on.

Follow-up possibility

Role play the situation and discuss any points of conflict.

Note: the same picture can be used for any current controversial issue.

472 *Profile Mobiles*

Students can create mobiles that contain descriptive words pertinent to a particular person. For example, a profile of Lincoln drawn on tag-board might be distributed. Each student then enters 'describing words' on individual 5″ × 8″ index cards and then strings them to the profile. Have each student explain why they chose specific words. With younger students, hand out a list of words from which they can make a selection.

Activities Note

The following Activities involving student feelings and reactions should also be considered as viable possibilities for carrying out instructional evaluation.

473 *Learning Logs*

At the end of each week, students complete the sentence:
"This week in social studies I learned that _____."

Call on individuals to share their statements.

474 *Word Check List*

After a particular topic or unit of study is completed, distribute a list of descriptive words and phrases (an example of one list is given below). Have the students circle those words and phrases that indicate their reactions.

Word Check List

For me, the topic (*name one just completed*):

    Was fun
    Was exciting
    Was boring
    Was OK
    Was interesting
    Is worth going on with
    Helped me think differently

Helped me feel differently about _____
Should be taught to other kids my age
Didn't last long enough
Was too long

475 *Rating Scales*

This activity is a modification of the *Word Check List* in Activity 474.

Students are asked to mark their reactions along a continuum of possibilities as shown in Figure 475.

Example

On each line, place an X that shows how you felt about our unit on Communication which we just finished.

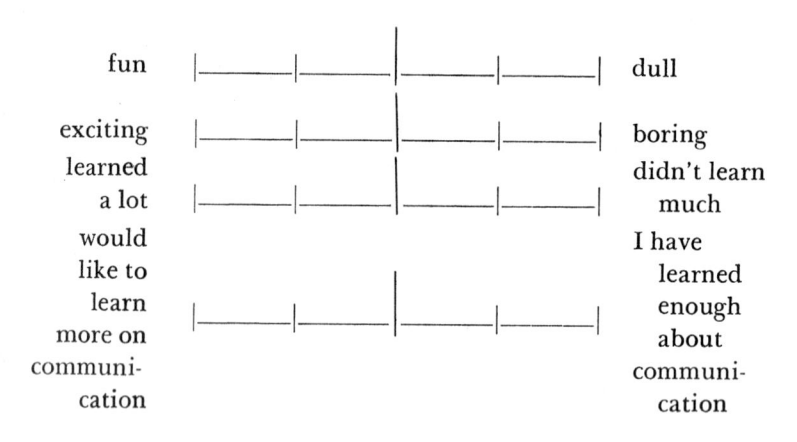

fun	|———|———|———|———|	dull
exciting	|———|———|———|———|	boring
learned a lot	|———|———|———|———|	didn't learn much
would like to learn more on communication	|———|———|———|———|	I have learned enough about communication

Figure 475

476 *Rank Ordering*

With this technique, students rank the various activities and topics with which they have been involved.

Example

We have just finished a unit on communication. Listed below are some of the things we did. Put a *1* in front of the activity you like the most, a *2* next to your second choice, a *3* for your next choice, and a *4* beside your last choice.

_____ Interviewed a blind person and a deaf person.
_____ Saw films on how people in other cultures communicated with gestures.
_____ Read books and pamphlets on communication.
_____ Communicated for one hour in our classroom without speaking.

✿ 477 *Individual Ranking*

This technique is an alternative to the *Rank Order* procedure in Activity 476.

The students react to each entry separately, rather than in comparison with other items on the list.

Example

We have just finished a unit on communication. Listed below are some of the things we did. For *each* item listed, circle a *1* if you thought it was a good activity, a *2* if you thought it was OK, and a *3* if you did not care for the activity.

Interviewed a blind person and a deaf person . . .	1	2	3
Saw films on how people in other cultures communicated with gestures	1	2	3
Read books and pamphlets on communication . .	1	2	3
Communicated for one hour in our classroom without speaking	1	2	3

478 Attitudinal Ordering

Notice the variation below for the *Individual Ranking* technique, Activity 477.

Example

> Read each of the following statements. Then, circle the *1* if you *really* agree, a *2* if you mostly agree, and a *3* if you *definitely* disagree.

It was fun studying about communication	1 2 3
I learned quite a lot during this study of communication	1 2 3
Other students my age would also enjoy studying about communication	1 2 3

479 Self-Evaluation

Have students collect their work into folders. At the end of a period of time (such as one week) have the students review their work and then complete a simple self-evaluation like the one in the following example.

Example

1. List several things you did especially well.

   _____

   _____

2. List several things that would make your work even better.

   _____

   _____

3. Circle *one* of the following:

   I think the work I have just looked at is:

   Excellent   Very Good   OK
   Needs Improvement

Attempt to review the self-evaluation sheets with each student, integrating your own assessment of the work into the dialogue.

CROSS-INDEX OF ACTIVITIES

In lieu of a traditional index, I have prepared this Cross-Index of Activities. Since all of the activities in this book are numbered sequentially, the reader can easily locate any and all activities that pertain to a given topic.

F.L.R.

Area	Activity Number
Anthropology/Sociology	3, 7, 8, 18, 42, 54, 57, 62, 66, 67, 71, 72, 77, 84, 86, 87, 88, 89, 90, 91, 92, 94, 95, 101, 115, 142, 145, 148, 149, 200, 202, 206, 211, 250, 251, 257, 296, 407
Awareness of Others	1, 21, 45, 54, 57, 75, 90, 91, 92, 93, 95, 99, 144, 148, 151, 153, 205, 209, 220, 233, 240, 242, 256, 265, 266, 267, 272,

CROSS-INDEX OF ACTIVITIES 299

Area	Activity Number
Awareness of Others (*Continued*)	282, 315, 385, 386, 393, 406, 439, 440, 446, 447, 449, 462, 463, 464, 465, 466, 468, 469, 470
Classifying	20, 21, 22, 23, 24, 25, 26, 27, 28, 29, 30, 31, 32, 33, 34, 35, 36, 37, 38, 40, 123, 135, 173, 244, 252, 253, 254, 275, 331, 348, 354
Comparing	3, 8, 14, 39, 40, 41, 42, 43, 44, 45, 46, 47, 48, 49, 51, 52, 53, 54, 55, 75, 76, 81, 108, 164, 172, 187, 195, 198, 212, 213, 214, 237, 255, 262, 287, 312, 326, 360, 367, 379, 413, 414, 420, 423
Conflict/Conflict Resolution	207, 209, 210, 211, 434, 471
Creating	11, 46, 59, 177, 189, 191, 201, 236, 238, 239, 243, 247, 250, 251, 277, 284, 288, 291, 292, 293, 295, 340, 343, 344, 345, 356, 365, 371
Data Analysis	73, 78, 81, 85, 96, 108, 109, 110, 111, 135, 137, 138, 258, 312, 324, 354, 370, 377, 414, 415, 417, 419
Data Collection	3, 17, 78, 81, 86, 87, 88, 125, 130, 132, 133, 142, 143, 145,

300   CROSS-INDEX OF ACTIVITIES

Area	Activity Number
Data Collection (*Continued*)	147, 148, 149, 150, 151, 161, 175, 200, 202, 212, 217, 222, 226, 229, 258, 293, 301, 310, 312, 313, 314, 319, 320, 322, 323, 324, 330, 337, 341, 352, 354, 358, 372, 373, 375, 376, 380, 400, 401, 402, 412, 441, 449, 451, 454, 455
Data Displays/Guides	6, 57, 70, 74, 78, 81, 82, 85, 89, 128, 133, 135, 154, 155, 160, 170, 171, 185, 215, 217, 222, 226, 230, 258, 266, 272, 301, 322, 330, 352, 378, 386, 391, 392, 418, 439, 458
Data Interpretation	3, 4, 73, 75, 78, 81, 83, 86, 87, 97, 108, 127, 135, 175, 179, 183, 221, 222, 226, 242, 268, 310, 312, 313, 319, 320, 322, 324, 330, 352, 354, 377, 378, 391, 392, 441, 442, 444, 445, 449
Data Processing	97, 108, 109, 110, 111, 137, 138, 139, 140, 141, 154, 155, 156, 157, 158, 161, 175, 190
Economics	309, 310, 311, 312, 313, 314, 315, 316, 317, 318, 319, 321, 322, 323, 324, 328, 349, 379
Evaluation	15, 16, 46, 79, 117, 118, 119, 120, 130, 134, 138, 175, 189, 201, 213, 218, 219, 223, 224,

CROSS-INDEX OF ACTIVITIES

Area	Activity Number
Evaluation (*Continued*)	230, 251, 299, 324, 325, 334, 473, 474, 475, 476, 477, 478, 479
Feelings, Attitudes	1, 17, 44, 75, 99, 102, 106, 144, 151, 153, 209, 240, 242, 263, 264, 267, 269, 272, 282, 336, 391, 392, 402, 405, 410, 456, 461, 465, 467, 473, 474, 475, 476, 477, 478
Geography	58, 60, 61, 69, 70, 82, 83, 136, 172, 173, 174, 175, 176, 177, 178, 179, 180, 181, 182, 183, 184, 185, 186, 304, 374, 382, 384, 394, 395, 421, 422, 453, 460
Graphing	154, 155, 160, 161, 202, 378
History	48, 49, 76, 100, 141, 151, 166, 187, 188, 189, 190, 191, 192, 208, 237, 255, 261, 262, 285, 303, 346, 364, 398, 411
Imagining	50, 151, 199, 201, 243, 260, 269, 273, 281, 283, 286, 291, 294, 298, 303, 305, 306, 307, 347, 390, 407, 452, 459
Inferring	18, 19, 22, 31, 32, 41, 54, 55, 57, 58, 63, 75, 77, 78, 79, 80,

CROSS-INDEX OF ACTIVITIES

Area	Activity Number
Inferring (*Continued*)	81, 82, 83, 84, 85, 86, 87, 144, 242, 254, 259, 322, 374, 391
Interest Centers	14, 24, 46, 117, 120, 165
Learning	66, 103, 114, 115, 199, 220, 221, 222, 223, 224, 227, 228, 231, 256, 258, 387, 388, 389, 396, 408, 473, 474, 475, 476, 477, 478, 479
Listening	137, 195, 196, 197, 198, 249
Maps, Globes	172, 173, 174, 175, 176, 177, 178, 179, 183
Observing	1, 2, 3, 4, 5, 6, 7, 8, 9, 10, 11, 12, 13, 14, 15, 16, 17, 18, 19, 20, 21, 42, 46, 57, 76, 142, 144, 145, 146, 197, 200, 202, 206, 217, 223, 226, 234, 248, 271, 329, 358, 378, 446, 454
Predicting	5, 55, 56, 57, 58, 59, 60, 61, 62, 63, 64, 66, 67, 68, 69, 70, 71, 72, 73, 74, 75, 81, 87, 89, 90, 91, 92, 93, 94, 95, 107, 112, 113, 114, 115, 116, 117, 118, 119, 120, 121, 130, 151, 289, 290, 292, 294, 297, 298, 301, 341, 401, 416

CROSS-INDEX OF ACTIVITIES

Area	Activity Number
Presenting/Information	135, 162, 163, 164, 165, 166, 167, 168, 169, 170, 171, 182, 192, 198, 366
Problem Solving	175, 181, 184, 208, 211, 231, 250, 251, 316, 332, 349, 406, 435
Questioning	151, 161, 163, 168, 198, 299, 433
Reporting	162, 163, 164, 165, 166, 167, 168, 169, 171, 198
Researching	71, 72, 74, 87, 88, 89, 90, 91, 92, 93, 94, 95, 96, 97, 98, 99, 100, 101, 102, 103, 104, 105, 106, 107, 112, 113, 114, 115, 116, 117, 118, 119, 120, 121, 122, 142, 143, 148, 149, 150, 151, 175, 179, 180, 200, 206, 217, 223, 226, 228, 266, 295, 310, 311, 319, 322, 330, 337, 346, 378, 380, 402, 441, 444, 445, 449
Role Playing/ Dramatization	162, 164, 166, 184, 208, 211, 258, 305, 332, 471
Self-Awareness	42, 75, 102, 104, 106, 145, 151, 160, 202, 209, 220, 221, 222, 263, 264, 267, 269, 272,

304 CROSS-INDEX OF ACTIVITIES

Area	Activity Number
Self-Awareness (*Continued*)	297, 300, 301, 308, 336, 351, 361, 402, 462, 465, 466, 467, 470, 473, 474, 475, 476, 477, 478, 479
Selling	134, 218, 318, 366, 425
Substantiating	25, 43, 52, 180, 185
Summarizing	44, 191, 192, 198, 222, 229, 269
Teaching	224, 225, 226, 230, 231, 267, 405, 409
Time Lines/Circles	65, 187, 188, 189, 192, 259